To Harold L. Raush
and
Robert L. Weiss

*whose excellent work has
stimulated our own research*

A Couple's Guide to COMMUNICATION

JOHN GOTTMAN
CLIFF NOTARIUS · JONNI GONSO
HOWARD MARKMAN

RESEARCH PRESS
2612 NORTH MATTIS AVENUE
CHAMPAIGN, IL 61822
(800) 519-2707
www.researchpress.com

23 22 21 20   07 08

ISBN 0-87822-127-1
Library of Congress Catalog Number 76-23968

CONTENTS

PREFACE FOR THE COUPLE

The skills presented here are based, in part, on a series of studies on how distressed and nondistressed couples differ when solving problems. We have now completed twelve studies with 250 couples.

A Couple's Guide to Communication is an interim product of this research. It differs from other books currently available in several ways. First, it is not based on our idealized conceptions of a good marriage, but on our studies of how intact, mutually satisfying marriages function in problem-solving situations. Second, it is written for you, the couple, and not for the professional. Third, it is concrete and specific. Instead of telling you to "communicate better" or to "try harder," we give you specific skills to improve communication. Fourth, these skills are based on our "task analysis" of what nondistressed couples do to solve *their* problems. We've invented devices that we think make the job easier, and that should make success more likely.

Three of the studies we did involved the evaluation of the materials that form this book. When evaluating these materials, two things have to be demonstrated: first, that these materials do teach the skills they claim to teach; second, that this makes a difference in marital satisfaction. We have evidence that the materials are effective for most couples, but we would like to stress that they cannot solve all your personal problems. However, if you are willing to work, we think that you can make some gains using these materials. That is all we promise.

We will revise and improve this material as we learn more about how to help couples solve problems. The book was developed on the basis of research, and it will be improved by further research. We think this is the best the field presently has to offer you.

PREFACE FOR THE PROFESSIONAL

This preface will give some context for the work that has formed the basis of the interventions contained in this book. Following is a brief review of the literature and our own work. Reprints, preprints, or unpublished technical reports can be obtained from our laboratory.*

Psychological research in family interaction has an interesting history. During World War II an interdisciplinary study group was formed by the army to design a gun that would follow and anticipate its target. The concepts of cybernetics, feedback and feedforward control, and the mathematics of stochastic time series analysis came out of that project. Although these concepts were initially applied to the study of neuronal networks, Norbert Wiener, a member of the group, soon saw the possibility for a general application of cybernetic concepts in the behavioral sciences. In 1946 the Macy Foundation sponsored a conference to which Gregory Bateson was invited. Ten years later Bateson, Jackson, Haley, and Weakland proposed the double-bind theory of schizophrenia.

Interaction in families was proposed as causally related to psychopathology and, presumably, this systemic view of families was also proposed as influential in maintaining psychopathology in the family member who was

* Department of Psychology, University of Illinois, Children's Research Center, 511 E. Gerty Street, Champaign, Illinois 61820

the "weak link" or "identified patient." The famous double-bind example that Bateson et al. (1956) described was the mother visiting her schizophrenic son in the hospital. The mother's body was stiff as her son hugged her; when he pulled away from her, she responded by saying, "What's the matter, aren't you glad to see your mother?" He is damned if he does and damned if he doesn't respond to her. Much earlier Sigmund Freud had described a story of the mother who bought her son two ties and, when he wore one tie the following day, the mother said, "What's the matter, you don't like the other tie?"

Although there is still debate about the double-bind hypothesis, research has generally indicated that, while it is true that families with a schizophrenic member exhibit channel inconsistency in message transmission, so do normal families. Despite the fact that the double-bind hypothesis has not been fruitful in the study of the etiology of schizophrenia, its study has had some interesting side effects.

One effect of the interest in the interaction of "schizophrenic families" has been the stimulation of interest in the social interaction of distressed families for its own sake. Clinicians have found it useful to work directly with the interacting system that is the focus of concern, and it is precisely in our clinical work with interacting systems that we have realized a great need for descriptive information.

Most of the description we have of interacting families initially came from the provocative ramblings of clinicians who worked only with distressed families and never saw a nondistressed family other than (presumably) their own. Despite this lack of information about how nondistressed couples and families function, we have created theoretical viewpoints on family pathology and fly-by-night therapy interventions. We are acting as if we know, for example, that positive reciprocity or the "Quid pro Quo" characterizes successful marriages—with no evidence. We believe in positive reciprocity primarily because first Lederer and Jackson (1968), then Richard Stuart (1969), and then Nathan Azrin (Azrin, Naster & Jones, 1973), and now the whole brass ensemble is out playing the "Quid pro Quo March." The work we began several years ago was simply an attempt *to describe systematically* what it is that nondistressed couples do differently than distressed couples to resolve marital conflict, and how they themselves perceive the messages they exchange.

THE PROBLEMS OF MARRIAGE

From the early 1950's sociologists like Strodtbeck (1951) have been focusing on marital decision making and conflict resolution. This seems intuitively appealing and sensible, but it has by no means been demonstrated that behavior during conflict resolution situations is what really counts in creating a satisfying marriage.

If you place an ad in a newspaper asking people to come into your laboratory if they feel their marriage is mutually satisfying, and then compare them to couples seeking marital counseling, you will be surprised (or perhaps not) to discover that both groups have precisely the same set of problems; in fact, the rank order of these problems in perceived severity is nearly identical. The two groups differ in how severe they perceive their problems to be, but marriages seem to have a fairly uniform set of problems to cope with. Mitchell, Bullard and Mudd (1962) described this phenomenon, and in our own data the rank order correlation using a standard problem inventory between distressed and nondistressed couples is about .94.

The measurement of marital satisfaction has a 40-year history in sociology that has included longitudinal research with 1,000 engaged couples (Burgess & Cottrell, 1939), an 18-year longitudinal study of married couples (Uhr, 1957), and many large-sample, cross-sectional studies (see Burgess, Locke & Thomes, 1971). Two major conclusions have emerged from this work:

1. Inventories to measure "happiness," "adjustment," "distress," "satisfaction," etc., all seem to be tapping

the same factor, which we refer to as "satisfaction."

2. The Locke-Wallace Marital Relationship Inventory (MRI) (Burgess, Locke & Thomes, 1971) emerges as the single best, short questionnaire measure which discriminates clinic from nonclinic marriages and correlates highly with inventories that have moderate degrees of validity in predicting marital stability.

To reduce heterogeneity in the kinds of couples studied, it would seem wise to use the convergence of two measurement operations in conjunction (see also Birchler, Weiss & Vincent, 1975, p. 351). In our investigations distressed couples were clinic couples at least one of whom was dissatisfied (low on the Locke-Wallace MRI); non-distressed couples were nonclinic couples both of whom were satisfied (high on the Locke-Wallace MRI). Cutoff scores on the MRI were those recommended by Burgess et al. (1971, pp. 330-331).

The sociological literature is not very theoretical or descriptive of how distressed marriages function, or of how that functioning differs from the way nondistressed marriages function. Perhaps the most promising theoretical language we have available to begin such a description is behavior exchange theory (Thibaut & Kelley, 1959).

If you look at behavior exchange theory carefully, you will find that the theory is not very clear on how payoffs are defined in a behavior exchange matrix. We know that person A exhibits behavior a_i and person B exhibits behavior b_j, and that this exchange has payoff p_{ij} to person A and payoff p'_{ij} to person B. Is the payoff a function of *exhibiting* the behavior as Gergen (1969) suggested, or of *receiving* a behavior, or both? Thibaut and Kelley (1959) suggested that a central concept in determining payoff was the "comparison level for alternative relationships," CL_{ALT}. This means that in some relationships a wife can do something that will be unappreciated because a husband's comparison level is high, whereas that same behavior will be strongly appreciated by a husband who does not think he can do better in alternative relationships.

Clearly, then, one way of interpreting the payoff matrix is that in a satisfying dyadic relationship each member *receives* behaviors that he or she codes as positive. This includes CL_{ALT} into the notion of payoff, and presumably the same behaviors could be coded as being positive or negative, depending on the receiver's CL_{ALT}.

Standard game theory experiments in which the experimenter restricts the behavioral repertoire of the interacting couple (to "compete" or "cooperate," for example), and in which the experimenter selects the payoff matrix, have not met with success in discriminating distressed from nondistressed couples (Speer, 1972). However, a study by Birchler, Weiss and Vincent (1975), in which observers coded the couples' behaviors as positive or negative, and in which the behavioral repertoire of the couple was not restricted, has been able to discriminate between distressed and nondistressed couples.

The first two studies we will describe involve the couple, not strangers coding their own behavior as positive or negative. There are several interesting implications to having the couple code their behavior. First, the procedure seems to be more consistent with behavior exchange theorizing. A smile may be a smirk to a spouse, or an interruption may display interest. When we get reliability between observers, we may be tapping into cultural stereotypes of marital behavior and ignoring the private, nonverbal message system that couples create from a long history of interaction. Second, it may be important to assess the extent to which spouses and strangers are consistent in their power to discriminate distressed from nondistressed couples. Third, an interesting question raised by the couple coding the partner's behavior is the viability of a communication deficit explanation of marital distress.

If distressed couples are likely to send messages that they *intend* their spouses to code negative, and they in fact *are* likely to be coded as negative, then they are communicating well. Their messages are coded as they intended. It would therefore make sense to have spouses code how they intend their own behavior to be taken by their partners.

So we built a device we call the "talk table" to make it possible for spouses to code the positivity of behavior received and the intended positivity of behavior exhibited as they interact.

A potential source of inconsistent results in the literature on family and couples interaction is the nature of the decision making task. Most researchers pay little attention to the task they select for families and couples to work on (Haley, 1964, 1967). There is evidence that there is some stability to talk and interruption patterns of three-person families, at least when they work on low conflict tasks such as telling a story using TAT cards (Jacob & Davis, 1973). One task dimension that has not been systematically studied is the level of conflict induced by the task. Some researchers (Olson & Ryder, 1970) have constructed tasks that induce a high level of conflict, while others (Jacob & Davis, 1973) use tasks that induce a low level of conflict. It may be important to know if distressed couples are different from nondistressed couples regardless of the level of conflict the task induces, or if they are only different on high conflict tasks.

We did two studies with the talk table because, although some reviews of the literature repeatedly recommend replication (Riskin & Faunce, 1972; Jacob, 1975), replication and extension of results is an uncommon practice. The sample of couples in the first study was from the university community at Indiana; the sample of couples from the second study was drawn from two non-university communities. The couples in the second study had been married about six-and-one-half years longer than the couples in the first study, and there was more variability in their educational levels.

Couples in both studies made decisions on high and low conflict tasks. In the first study there were three low conflict tasks: (1) a consensual ranking of dog breeds in terms of preference (Haley, 1964); (2) a story constructed using three TAT cards (Locke, 1961); and (3) a consensual rank ordering of items for their survival value on the moon

(Hall, 1971). The high conflict tasks were: (1) The Inventory of Marital Conflict (Olson & Ryder, 1970), and (2) a discussion of an actual, unresolved marital problem. To facilitate the discussion of an existing marital problem, and to build rapport with the couple, an interviewing team discussed the couple's responses to a problem inventory. The couple had individually filled out the problem inventory and, following the interview, selected a salient problem. They were instructed to come to a mutually satisfying resolution of this problem.

CODING RESULTS

We found that distressed husbands were coding 36% of their wives' behavior as positive, whereas nondistressed husbands were coding 57% of their wives' behavior as positive. This same pattern held for the wife's coding of her husband's behavior, and this result was consistent for both studies. The F-ratios were larger in the second study.

There were essentially no differences in *intent* across both studies for husbands and wives. This supports a communication deficit explanation of marital distress. Distressed couples were having less positive impact on their spouses than they intended.

These results are consistent with the findings of Birchler et al. (1975) for observers' coding of couples' behavior on a high conflict task (the Olson and Ryder Inventory of Marital Conflict task used in this investigation). We found that the talk table is an inexpensive way to study behavior exchange in marriages, especially compared to detailed ratings of video tapes as in Birchler et al. (1975). The talk table variables are capable of discriminating distressed from nondistressed couples with a power greater than that obtained by the Birchler et al. (1975) ratings of video tapes.

CONFLICT RESULTS

To study the effects of induced conflict, the five talk-table buttons were treated as a 5-point Likert scale (1 = super negative to 5 = super positive), and Impact and Intent scores were averaged separately across high and low conflict tasks.

Surprisingly, Study 1 showed that it was equally easy to discriminate distressed from nondistressed couples regardless of the level of conflict the task induced. This is remarkable when one looks at the tasks, which vary from ranking a set of dog breeds to resolving a personal problem. In the second study, however, it was possible to discriminate the two groups only on the high conflict tasks. Perhaps these results account for the inconsistent findings in family interaction literature. More reliable results might be obtained by using only high conflict tasks.

The fact that the couples in Study 2 were married longer may account for the obtained differences on the conflict-by-group interaction effects in the two studies. Perhaps distressed couples who have been married longer have learned to avoid disagreement and exchange more positive messages in low conflict situations than distressed couples who are more recently married. This hypothesis is consistent with the clinical picture of the "stable-unsatisfactory" marriage in which couples present a happy, united front in most social situations.

RECIPROCITY
Reciprocity of positive exchange has been repeatedly implicated as the single most important description of good marriages in the clinical literature (Azrin, Naster & Jones, 1973; Lederer & Jackson, 1968; Rappaport & Harrell, 1972; Stuart, 1969; Weiss, Hops & Patterson, 1973).

It is important to point out that high base rates of positive codes for both husband and wife are not equivalent to reciprocity. Although nondistressed couples may seem to be reciprocating positive codes more frequently than distressed couples, that may only be an artifact of the higher probability of positive codes in nondistressed couples. What needs to be demonstrated is that significant reduction in uncertainty is gained about a particular consequent code in a sequence by knowledge of a particular antecedent code. For example, the conditional probability of a consequent positive wife code W+, given an antecedent positive husband code H+, must be significantly greater than the nonconditional probability of occurrence of W+. This means that a knowledge of the antecedent code H+ adds significantly to the ability to predict the occurrence of a W+ code over and above prediction from simply knowing the relative frequency of occurrence of W+. Symbolically, what must be demonstrated in this example is that $p(W+/H+) > p(W+)$. This has never been demonstrated in the literature on couples' interaction.

The distinction between high rates of positive codes and reciprocity has been ignored in the clinical literature on family interaction. For example, Alexander (1973) found that the correlation across families between parent-to-child supportive behavior and child-to-parent supportive behavior was significantly different from zero (father/son $R = .69$, $p < .05$; mother/son $r = .59$, $p < .05$). Although these correlations may indicate similarity in the rates of occurrence of supportive behaviors, the correlations do not imply contingent immediate reciprocity. A family with high rates of supportiveness could be distributing these behaviors noncontingently throughout a discussion. In this case the correlations obtained would be high as a function of different base rates across families, but there would still be no evidence of temporal reciprocity.

The base rate/reciprocity issue is also important for distinguishing between behavior exchange and social learning theories of distressed versus nondistressed marital conflict resolution. Birchler et al. (1975) used a mix of language from both theories. They demonstrated that distressed couples emit lower rates of positive codes and higher rates of negative codes than nondistressed couples. This does not justify calling the positive codes "social reinforcements." It would be necessary to show that a particular code on the part of one spouse affects the probability of occurrence of a particular code of the other spouse.

The appropriate test of the positive reciprocity hypothesis is that the difference between the conditional and unconditional probabilities is greater in nondistressed than in distressed couples. An independent hypothesis is that *negative* reciprocity is greater in distressed than in nondistressed couples.

We essentially found no evidence that positive reciprocity discriminates between distressed and nondistressed couples in either of two studies.

In general, across two studies the data support a "bank account" model rather than a reciprocity model. Positive codes or "deposits" must exceed negative codes or "withdrawals." Perhaps it is precisely this lack of contingency in positive interaction that characterizes satisfying and stable nondistressed marriages. Nondistressed couples in the second study, who had been married longer than nondistressed couples in the first study, showed less reciprocity than nondistressed couples in the first study. In fact, in the interventions in this book we stress the concept that behavior change be "unlatched" or *not* contingent.

CODING COUPLES' INTERACTION

The third study described here is based on our coding video tapes of distressed and nondistressed couples resolving an existing personal problem. We owe a great deal of the impetus for our work to the pioneering research of Weiss and his associates. Our coding system was based, in part, on Weiss' Marital Interaction Coding System (MICS). In our system, however, one group of coders coded the content of each message unit on a verbatim transcript using 22 content codes that we lump into 8 summary content codes for analysis. These summary codes are: (1) Agreement, (2) Disagreement, (3) Mind reading, (4) Problem solving, (5) Problem talk/feeling, (6) Communication talk, (7) Summarizing self, and (8) Summarizing other.

Another group of coders used a hierarchical decision rule to code the nonverbal behavior of the speaker and listener during message delivery. The decision rule is derived from Albert Mehrabian's research on nonverbal communication (1972). A demarcated unit of transcript and video tape is first scanned for positive or negative facial expressions by looking down a list of key words.

Positive Face	Negative Face	
smile	frown	mocking laughter
laughter	sneer	smirk
empathic face	fear face	angry face
head nod	cry	disgust
eye contact	glare	

If there are no positive or negative facial cues, then voice tone cues are scanned using a set of key words.

Positive Voice		Negative Voice	
caring	satisfied	cold	blaming
warm	buoyant	tense	sarcastic
soft	bubbly	scared	angry
tender	cheerful	impatient	furious
relieved	chuckling	hard	blaring
empathic	happy	clipped	hurt
concerned	joyful	staccato	depressed
affectionate	laughing	whining	accusing
loving			

If there are no positive or negative facial or voice cues, then body position and movement cues are scanned.

Positive Body	Negative Body
touching	arms akimbo
distance reduction	neck or hand tension
open arms	rude gestures
attention	throw up hands in disgust
relaxation	point, jab
forward lean	inattention

The content/nonverbal behavior distinction is important for clearing up a strategic source of confusion when coding marital and family interaction. The confusion is between a description of a behavior and the function of a behavior in its context. For example, in the following sequence the wife's statement would usually be coded as a disagreement in the context following the husband's proposal because it apparently functions to disagree with the husband's idea of how to spend the vacation.

H: Let's spend Christmas at your mother's.
W: You always get tense at my mother's.

We code that message as a mind-reading statement (MR), by which we mean that she is attributing feelings (or thoughts, motives, and actions) to her husband. We have found that all couples mind read, but that the nonverbal delivery of the mind-reading statement determines whether it gets seen as a sensitive feeling probe or as a criticism. Couples do not ask about feelings in the way Carl Rogers would. Instead, they mind read with positive nonverbal cues. In this case, the MR is likely to be followed by agreement and elaboration of feelings. In the MR negative case, the mind reading is likely to be followed by disagreement and elaboration of feelings or Summarizing self.

RELIABILITY

Reliability between coders is generally low in this literature. There is a kind of tacit agreement that researchers will not tattle on one another about reliability. Reliability is usually inversely related to the complexity of the coding system used. Also, reliability depends on whether researchers do sequential data analysis. If sequential analysis is not interesting (as in Alexander, 1973), one can sum over blocks of interaction and calculate reliability as total inter-coder correlations. Sequential analysis requires stringent reliability calculations of agreement to agreement plus disagreement proportions tied to specific transcript units.

Transcript units vary from phrases to floor switches to entire pages of transcript (Riskin & Faunce, 1972). Summary codes often lump disparate content codes so that the summary codes are relatively meaningless. For example, Raush, Barry, Hertel and Swain (1974) combined "raising an issue," "seeking information," "withholding information," "agreeing with the other's statement," and "denying the validity of the other's argument with or without the use of counter arguments." This summary code was called "cognitive" by Raush et al. (1974). When content codes were not combined, reliabilities were in the 40's; they were in the 80's with the summary codes.

Our reliabilities for nonverbal behavior are approximately 85%, and the majority of our coders (we use ten coders) agree an average of 91% of the time, with the transcript unit as the reliability unit. We also control for decay and drift in our assessments of reliability.

The results indicate that content codes (except for agreement) do not discriminate well between distressed and nondistressed couples. However, when the content codes are combined with the nonverbal delivery codes, discrimination is powerful. Each of the major segments of this book is based on our results, the findings of other researchers (particularly the work of Harold Raush and his associates, and the work of Robert Weiss and his associates) and our own clinical experience. After a terminal behavioral objective was determined for each social skill we intend to teach a couple, we did a task analysis of the skill (Gagné, 1967), and wrote materials to maximize the couples' chances for success at each step in acquiring each skill. We would like to walk you through the book chapter by chapter to give you an idea of where the skills originated.

THE SOCIAL SKILLS
One of the basic ideas of this book is that therapy interventions are "unlatched" or noncontingent. This deals with a resistance to change that is familiar to marriage counselors (for example, see Stuart, 1969), namely, "I won't change until my spouse changes." Within that context, the following skills are taught:

1. *Listening and Validation* deals with reducing the proportion of summary statements that are Summarizing self (SS) and ending what we call the "SS Syndrome." The skill taught is Check-out and paraphrasing; the cognitive organizer is the Intent/Impact model which we get from our talk table studies.

Validation is a skill related to the higher frequency of "accepting" behaviors, such as assent and agreement (see Weiss et al., 1973), when one's spouse is expressing feelings. Validating a spouse's position does not usually imply agreement with the position to nondistressed couples, but rather communicates, "I can see how you think and feel that way, even if I don't see it the way you do."

The objective of this chapter is to enable couples to get feedback on Intent/Impact discrepancies, call a "Stop Action" when there is a discrepancy, and use the Interim Troubleshooting Guide to find an intervention (usually a listening and validation procedure) to improve communication. The chapter also begins to build a language of "marital games" which can be used as tags of specific behavior patterns so that the couple can monitor and intervene to change these patterns. Rather than teach couples directly to mind read with positive nonverbal behavior, we do it indirectly. We make them aware of mind reading as a way of attributing blame. We do not expect to eliminate mind reading, but we do expect to affect its nonverbal delivery.

2. *Leveling* is a skill to reduce mind reading (attributing feelings, thoughts, motives, behaviors) to the spouse, which distressed couples usually do with negative, nonverbal cues. Leveling reduces blaming. It is well known that distressed couples' complaints are general attacks on a spouse's character. The behavioral objective is to be able to transform such a general attack to a specific statement: "When you do X, in situation Y, I feel Z," so that this statement can become an agenda item.

To assist in this process, the feeling chart, assertion instructions, discussions of catastrophic expectations, and the suggestion box are methods based upon an analysis of the components of the leveling task from our knowledge of couples who have trouble leveling. These couples are the conflict avoiders who feel lonely, cut off, or who intellectualize feelings and issues. We also found that in nondistressed marriages the nonverbal behavior of the listener was more positive while the spouse was expressing feelings than in distressed marriages. This finding relates to our stress on being a good receiver of leveling statements (Chapter 2).

3. *Editing* is a skill designed for couples continually engaged in bickering or in escalating quarrels. For the extreme case, we wrote Chapter 7, "Getting Through a Crisis." For the nonextreme case, it is well known that even highly distressed couples are capable of being nice to strangers. This has been found in research (Ryder, 1968; Winter, Ferreira & Bowers, 1973; Halverson & Waldrop, 1970; Birchler, Weiss & Vincent, 1975), and is also a part of many books on etiquette (such as Eleanor Roosevelt's book).

   This chapter teaches couples to proofread their own behavior so that they can self-control escalating quarrels. They learn to "edit" the scripts of other couples, they learn nine rules of politeness, and then specific etiquette rules with one another (Chapter 7).

   Even for couples not engaged in escalating quarrels, editing works as a renewal process so that they can back off, act like strangers, get in touch, and level within a climate of positive or considerate behavior.

4. *Negotiating agreements* has the objective of identifying three parts of a "Family Meeting"—gripe time, agenda-building time, and problem-solving time. At the end of this segment, couples may still begin a Family Meeting with negative nebulous complaints, but they learn to change them into specific negative complaints (Leveling), and then into positive suggestions.

   To achieve closure on the Family Meeting, we

have the couple use the "Up deck," a deck of cards containing specific behaviors that they decide to increase in frequency. A contract is used to close the deal. This latter part of the family meeting using contracting is a common part of many behavior therapy approaches to couples and family therapy (Lederer & Jackson, 1968; Stuart, 1969; Azrin, Naster & Jones, 1973; Weiss, Hops & Patterson, 1973; Alexander, 1973). We find that nondistressed couples have more PL/AG sequences (where one person proposes a plan and the other agrees) and more AM (accepting modification of one's own position), and that these tend to occur in the last third of the discussion.

In fact, the first third of a discussion for distressed couples is characterized by more communication about communication (meta communication) statements than is true for nondistressed couples. We describe this in Chapter 5, "Hidden Agendas."

5. *Hidden Agendas* deals with wheel spinning in discussions and is related to an unstated issue of positiveness, responsiveness, or status (Mehrabian, 1972). It also begins to get at issues of closeness.

We have found that some couples who learn the first four skills will say something like, "The marriage is better, but it's still dull," or "I still feel cut off, lonely." Hidden agenda dimensions, when addressed, begin to get at these marital issues.

The next four chapters "Solving Your Sexual Problems," "Making a Good Thing Better," "Getting Through a Crisis," and "Getting Out of a Bad Marriage" go far beyond our own research. They are summaries of clinical activity and writing, although little research has been done in these areas. We do know something about what couples do to have fun and to spoil fun, and we've included some of our work with the "Fun deck" (Appendix E) in Chapter 8. However, for the most part, we are out on a limb in these chapters, and we say so. Future research in our laboratory will be directed toward these areas of closeness and marriage enhancement. Other aspects of the intervention program not discussed in this preface are based on our experiences with typical resistances to change we've encountered when using these materials (for example, this is why we discuss "catastrophic expectations" about change).

In Chapter 6, "Solving Your Sexual Problems," we have a modest goal: to inform couples about which procedures are currently available for sexual problems. Unfortunately, cases in sex clinics are heavily screened to rule out couples with communication problems, so we really do not currently know how effective the techniques would be for distressed marriages with sexual problems. We think, however, that it provides relief to know that psychologists consider sexual problems *as problems,* that is, capable of a solution. In our own data, we are amazed at how difficult *all couples* found it to discuss sexual matters with any frankness. Often we read halfway through a transcript before we realized that the couple was even discussing sex. So our goal in this chapter is simply to legitimize discussion of a topic couples avoid all too much—in effect, to open conversation about sexuality and sensuality.

Finally, we want to say that we were somewhat ambivalent about publishing these materials at this time. Much more work is necessary, and some of that work is in progress in our laboratory (and also, as far as we know, in Oregon, Massachusetts and Stony Brook). We finally decided that there are several reasons for these materials being made available now. They improve on what is currently available; they may stimulate further research; they open us up to criticism and, hopefully, will stimulate dialog about social skills training with couples. We think it makes sense to generate interventions empirically by finding out how couples deal with conflict, rather than by armchairing interventions. Finally, we consider this book a report of work in progress which we hope to be able to update as we learn more from couples. We are aware of the modesty of our contribution.

ACKNOWLEDGMENTS

This book was developed as part of a marital research project which has been primarily supported by a grant from the National Institute of Mental Health, Grant No. PHS ROI MH 2459, the Social Problems section.

We have had an active research laboratory with an enthusiastic staff that has done a tedious job of coding tapes carefully for several years. Shirley Taylor and Sue Hansen were intelligent and excellent secretaries who typed endless hours of verbatim transcripts. Nita Arnove, Lib Buck, Carla Comarella, Audrey Heller, and Coleen Turner have been the core of our staff. They have kept the lab reasonably together and made it a nice place to visit. They have been coders as well as couples' therapists. Many students have also helped with the coding of video and audio tapes.

We want to thank David Carrico, Gail Garber, Sherry Goldstein, Jerry Sinsabaugh, and Linda Stastney; they formed our first generation of coders on the Couples Inter-action Scoring System. We also want to acknowledge the contribution of people who consistently joined our staff for our many couples' workshops: Mary Anna Green, Barbara Moore, Armen Sarkessian, Sue Toler, Rosemary Trubitt, Milt Taliadoures and Debbie Brandon. We want to thank the Psychology Department of Indiana University and the Indiana University Foundation for providing continuing research support when it counted the most.

We are indebted to agencies in Bloomington, Indiana that provided support and referrals when we were beginning our research: the Mental Health Center, Student Health Services, the Center for Human Growth, the Center for Counseling and Psychological Services, and the Psychological Clinic. Finally, our greatest debt is to those couples who were willing to share with us what is most intimate and central to their lives. We hope that this contribution will make worthwhile the trust you put in us.

INTRODUCTION

You are about to begin a program for improving communication in your marriage. The program is designed so that you will progress in a step-by-step fashion, experiencing the maximum possible success at each step along the way. You can expect to make gains in your communication during this program. However, it is also important for you to realize that this program is intended to teach you skills that will *begin* a process of learning. This is similar to learning to drive a car. After most of us get a driver's license, we are not really good drivers. It usually takes several thousand miles of driving under a variety of road conditions to practice the driving skills we learned before we are really competent drivers. It is impossible to learn all the necessary skills at one time. At first you may learn how to drive in a parking lot, then on uncrowded streets, and finally in traffic. Similarly, the communication skills you first learn will not solve all of your problems. However, each skill will build upon those you've already learned. We only ask that you try to practice the skills throughout the program. At the beginning, you will still find yourself experiencing problems in your relationship that you seem unable to handle. The reason is that there are additional skills that you've *not yet learned* that will eventually help you to get through these problem points.

The first pitfall you will encounter is doing the things we recommend that may seem unspontaneous and phony.

We have found that some people experience this when first learning a new skill. And, in fact, you will need to tailor these new ways of acting so that they fit your personality, and your individual style. It's like buying a new pair of shoes that are cut in standard sizes. They are not really comfortable until you break them in. Then they will fit the contours of your foot. It's the same with new skills.

How much you profit from this program will be partly determined by the extent to which you practice and put into effect our various suggestions. We recommend that you adopt a new approach in this program: be experimental. Try a suggestion first before you evaluate it. Let experience be your teacher. Many of the things we suggest provide a great deal of relief from distress. However, some of them are good for some people but not for others.

TRY IT FIRST,
THEN EVALUATE IT.

Every problem has a solution. You may eventually think of a better solution than the one we suggest, but start with our suggestions.

SPECIAL NOTE FOR COUPLES
EXPERIENCING MARITAL DISTRESS

The major issue behind other issues for most couples is whether or not to stay together. Sometimes one spouse wants to stay together and try to improve the marriage, and the other does not. Often both will be ambivalent, and this may vary in a see-saw fashion over time. You will need to think about why you have decided to work on things, and what you would like to see happen. You need to reach some agreement about what you're working toward right now. It may be a "least common denominator" agreement. For example, suppose you say, "I want to move out and try life on my own. I just don't know that I want to stay together." Your spouse says, "I want to work on our relationship. I know it hasn't been good, but I think we can work on it." You'll need to find out how you react to the other's goals.

xxx

Usually, however, *both* husband and wife will have mixed feelings about staying together, ranging from optimism to despair. They want to try to make things work but are stuck at being able to solve their own problems. They've tried everything they know on their own and they haven't gotten anywhere. For such couples it is a matter of choice as to how the future of the marriage is to be viewed. This is like a gallon jug with half a gallon of wine in it; it can be viewed as half empty or half full. The perception of the relationship, however, *will* make a difference in how hard you work on change.

Two views are possible:

1. This marriage is like a sinking ship. Maybe it can be saved, but I doubt it. However, I am willing to try. But if it doesn't work out, I am getting out.
2. This marriage has real problems. It may not last, but I am going to work to make it last. I am willing to try. Obviously, if things don't work out, we will split up. But I am going to act as if it will last.

These two views are expressed continually by couples who are ambivalent about staying together: they are *alternative* perceptions.

Consider the second view. This way of thinking must be rehearsed, and you've got to watch yourself and how you act. People who take this view are more likely to talk about their future, even if only hypothetically.

We're going to ask you to think about making a temporary agreement with each other, to adopt the second view for a while. We do this because we think it will help a great deal if you do it as you read this book. You may think that this request is simple minded and maybe even offensive. Please don't. Our only purpose in suggesting an optimistic perspective is to increase the possibility that you will both work at trying the communication skills we suggest. If you don't choose to change your perspective on your marriage, then consider striking a temporary contract with each other to give the suggestions in this book a trial.

1 LISTENING AND VALIDATION

INTENT AND IMPACT

In this chapter you will essentially be learning the skill which we call "Listening and Validation." But first we'd like to discuss what we mean by communication, as it relates to **Intent** and **Impact**.

What is Communication?

We are going to suggest a very simple way of thinking about communication. Then we will suggest ways to *improve* communication.

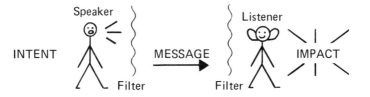

Intent and Impact Defined

In the above figure you see a speaker who has an *intention* of what he wants to communicate to the listener. He sends a *message,* and that message has an *impact* on the listener.

Good communication means having the impact you intended to have, that is, Intent equals Impact. In other words, good communication between intimates is clear and precise. The speaker tries to clarify the intent of his mes-

1

sage by stating exactly what he is thinking, wanting, or feeling. He does not assume the listener "knows" what is going on his head; he tells the listener so that the listener doesn't have to guess or mind read. The good listener tries to make sure that the intent of the message is understood, and does not fill in gaps with guesses as to what is going on in the speaker's mind. Both partners are trying to make sure that Intent equals Impact. Unfortunately, there are many times when Intent *does not* equal Impact, and many reasons why this is the case.

One reason is that the speaker's way of sending the message is inconsistent with his intent. The message must pass through the speaker's "filter" and come out in a particular way. For example, if you come home in a bad mood, you may say something to your spouse in a harsh way when actually you're mad at someone else. You may even be unaware of sounding cross.

Another reason why Intent does not equal Impact is that the listener may not hear the message the way it was delivered. The message must pass through the listener's "filter," and it can get distorted in the process. For example, if you are feeling depressed, a compliment may sound phony. It might have sounded sincere if you were in a better mood.

In any particular discussion with your spouse you need to find out *why* communication did not occur. The only way to do that is to get **Feedback**. *Feedback is what happens when the listener tells the speaker about the impact a message had.* But you have to *ask for* feedback. Only when you know the impact that the message actually had and compare it to your intent can you find out where miscommunication occurred. Unfortunately, most of us live in a feedback vacuum. We rarely get or ask for feedback; we simply always assume that Intent equals Impact, and this assumption leads to hurt feelings, confusion, or a variety of other communication pitfalls. The following conversation is an example and shows where it would have been helpful to request some feedback.

2

The first step in requesting feedback is to call a **Stop Action**. A Stop Action is a request you make for you and your spouse to talk over how you are feeling and to check Intents and Impacts.

Husband		Wife	
Unspoken Intent or Impact (He thinks)	*Spoken Message*	*Spoken Message*	*Unspoken Intent or Impact (She thinks)*
She's got a new sweater. I wonder if it is new. She looks good in it.			
	Is that a new sweater?	I got it on sale!	He thinks I'm a spendthrift!
Boy, is she nasty. Well, I have been denying myself a new pipe, sticking to our budget.	Where did you buy it?		
			I'm not putting up with this third degree police investigation!
		None of your business!	
I'll show her.	I'm going to buy a new pipe. I'll show you whose business it is!		
		I don't care what you do.	He certainly is childish.

Here is how the conversation might proceed if a Stop Action were to be called.

Husband		Wife	
Unspoken Intent or Impact (He thinks)	*Spoken Message*	*Spoken Message*	*Unspoken Intent or Impact (She thinks)*
She's angry at me. I wonder where we missed each other. What did I say that made her angry?	Hey, wait a minute! Stop the action! How are you feeling now?		He cares about me. He senses something has gone wrong
		I am feeling accused of spending too much money.	
Where did she get that? I didn't say that.	What did I say to give you that feeling?	It was your questioning me about the sweater. The way you kept asking questions.	Maybe he didn't mean to accuse me.
And I thought I was going to compliment her on the sweater. But she was so nasty.	I liked the way you looked in it and I just wondered if it was new.	I guess I was too sensitive to your questions.	
I'll check Intent/Impact.	I don't think you've been a spendthrift if that's what you felt I was saying.	I misunderstood then. I'm really glad you like my new sweater.	

4

You can see that a Stop Action can break a long cycle of miscommunication in which Intents do not match Impacts. In this way you can prevent a conversation from running away from you when you don't know why things are getting out of hand.

Messages

It is important for you to realize that all messages have two components: a *Content* component, which is the printed word meaning of the message, and a *Feeling* component, which is how the content is delivered. What are the feelings you hear behind the content of the message? Take the message, "You promised Billy that I would take him to a baseball game." This message could be delivered with several different feeling components. For example:

Content	*Feeling*
1. *You* promised Billy that I would take him to a baseball game!	I can't believe that you would have the nerve to promise him that I would do something.
2. You *promised* Billy that I would take him to a baseball game.	I think it is really important to keep a promise.
And so on. . . .	

A particular content could be said nonverbally in various ways. Each way conveys a different feeling and gives the content a different meaning. The feeling could be surprise, disgust, anger, hurt, sadness, joy, or any blend of feelings. The point is that you need to be aware of both aspects of the message. See if you can summarize both components of your spouse's messages.

Exercise 1   The Floor Exercise

It will help your communication a great deal if you use the following methods.

First, decide on an issue you will discuss. Use the *Problem Inventory* to select an issue you want to work on (see Appendix A, pp. 178-181); there is one for the husband and one for the wife. You should fill them out separately and

5

then compare them and agree on an issue to talk about.

Second, take an index card and label it like the following:

The Floor

You may have heard the expression "You have the floor." This means that the person who has the floor can speak. When that person is finished speaking, he hands over the card marked "The Floor" and this is called a floor switch. We suggest that you use this procedure for this exercise. If your spouse has the Floor and you want to speak, you have to ask for the Floor.

To facilitate feedback, take two index cards and label them as follows:

Positive   Negative

Any time you are listening and your partner has the Floor, you can hold up either one of these cards to show the impact of the message. This may or may not lead to an immediate floor switch.

If there are too many negative impacts, or if you don't understand a negative impact, it would be wise to call a Stop Action and get some feedback on whether Intent equals Impact. Try to detect the feeling as well as the content of the feedback you get.

THE SUMMARIZING SELF SYNDROME

A problem we've seen repeatedly with couples is the Summarizing Self Syndrome (the SS Syndrome). Here is a typical conversation between a husband (H) and wife (W) in this syndrome:

H: Blah Blah
W: Yak Yak
H: What I said was "Blah Blah"
W: What I said was "Yak Yak"

H: But don't you see that I am saying "Blah Blah"?
W: You won't even recognize that I have already said "Yak Yak"
H: How blind can you be?
W: Who's blind around here?

You can fill in the "Blah Blah" or the "Yak Yak" with anything you like. The point is that each person continues restating his or her own position. It's as if they each think "If only she (he) would see how logical my point is and how much sense it makes to see things the way I see them, we wouldn't have any problems." Each person is so sure he or she is right that they both think it's a waste of time to try to hear and understand the other person's viewpoint. "What's the use of listening to that old, stupid, wrong, idiotic, pigheaded, stubborn point of view my spouse has?" And so neither person really listens. They both just restate again and again. And they both feel frustrated, not listened to, not respected, put down, and lonely.

Below are some indicators of the Early Stages of the SS Syndrome. You may have gone through some of these stages on some issues. We will list several new terms under the various stages of the SS Syndrome which we will explain later. These terms will help you to diagnose the effects of the SS Syndrome.

Early Stages of the SS Syndrome
1. Both feel hurt and not listened to.
2. Neither feels that the other sees his or her point of view.
3. Conversation keeps seeming to drift "Off Beam."
4. Can't seem to stay on a topic long enough to solve it.
5. "Mind reading."
6. "Kitchen sinking."

Off Beam
Sometimes the problems, needs, and wishes that you and your partner have seem to tangle up like one big knot so that when you are discussing one problem area with each other, you keep drifting into other problem areas. Instead of resolving *any* of the problems, you just get more and more tired and frustrated. Below are several examples.

7

Mr. and Mrs. Bill Miller have a tennis match with one of Bill's out-of-town business associates and his wife. Mrs. Miller agreed to meet Bill in front of the racquet club. She arrived 20 minutes late. Bill waited for her while the other couple warmed up.

H: Why were you late?

W: I tried my best. The traffic was . . .

H: Yeah? You and who else? Your mother was always late, too.

W: Oh, come on.

H: You're just as sloppy as she is.

W: You don't say! Who's picking whose dirty underwear off the floor every morning?

H: I happen to go to work. What have *you* got to do all day?

W: I'm trying to get along on the money you don't make, that's what.

H: Why should I work for someone as selfish as you?

The Millers got very little out of this encounter except a thoroughly spoiled tennis match and evening. Below is a different kind of situation:

H: This Christmas let's spend equal time with both parents.

W: That seems so mechanical.

H: Last year we wound up spending most of it with your folks.

W: It is very hard being around your mother. You know that.

H: Well, I just get caught in the middle between you two. Why can't you just ignore the dumb things she says?

W: Because from the first she was against our getting married.

H: But now she's not that bad. I admit she's mean at times, but you're pretty unreasonable too.

W: And all that pressure she puts on us now to have babies.

H: Well, I would like a baby, too. You can't blame her for wanting to be a grandmother.

W: I'm going to have a career and that is that.

This couple has a habit of rambling from one issue to another instead of sticking to one problem. What they need to do is get the conversation "back on beam." Here is another couple's discussion:

W: I guess the main problem is that we don't have enough time to spend with one another.

8

H: Right, but more than that we can't agree on what to do when we do have time to be together.

W: Well, what about the time we both wanted to see the new movie at the Von Lee theatre.

H: Well, what about it?

W: Hey, don't get that way—whenever we talk about this you seem to get impatient. That's why we never go anywhere—we spend all our time arguing.

H: That's not true; we don't argue as much as other couples. In fact, we probably argue much less. For instance, look at Bobby Joe and Betty Lou. They fight all the time. . . .

Notice that the couple has strayed from the original problem. Instead of talking about how to arrange their schedule so that they can spend more time together (an effective problem-solving strategy), they are now discussing how much they argue. How can the couple get back on topic? Here is an example:

W: (interrupting) We're not talking about other couples. We're talking about us—and our problem is not how much we argue, but that we have little time to spend with each other. So let's get back to this problem, OK?

The wife has brought the conversation "back on beam" and they can now discuss the issue. Another indicator of the early stages of the SS Syndrome is the "mind-reading act."

Mind Reading
As we get to know another person very well, we often act as if we can "read the other person's mind." This habit can lead to a great deal of miscommunication where Intent does not equal Impact. The dialog below is an example:

H: I know you like romantic-type movies, so I made arrangements to go to see the new picture in town tonight—I'm sure you'll like it.

W: There you go again, making plans without consulting me. And besides, it's insulting that you think I'd like every romantic-sounding movie that comes out of Hollywood.

The husband is doing what we call **Mind Reading** because

he is assuming three things without first checking with his wife. His three mind-reading assumptions are: (1) she likes all romantic movies; (2) she'd like to see a movie on this particular evening; (3) she'd like to see this particular movie.

In this case the husband acted on his mind-reading assumption, much to his wife's dismay. However, mind reading can also occur when a couple is having a discussion.

W: What do you want to do tonight?
H: Oh, nothing. Let's stay home.
W: Well, OK, but I really would like to get out of the house.
H: Well, you're tired tonight. We'll do something tomorrow.

Did you spot the mind reading? It occurred in the husband's last statement. He assumes his wife is tired without asking her.

We're now ready for a more formal definition of mind reading. Mind reading occurs whenever one person assumes what another person is either feeling or thinking without asking. Mind reading is a short cut in communication because it avoids the added steps of asking the other person how he or she feels or thinks about a particular person or event (including themselves). Since it is almost impossible to actually know what another person feels or thinks without asking, our attempts at mind reading are often wrong and result in problems.

Below is a dialog to demonstrate how mind-reading acts can be changed to improve communication. *Remember that mind reading can be replaced by directly asking your spouse how he or she feels or thinks.*

H1: What's the problem with the house?
W1: You don't like to help me clean.
H2: That's not the problem at all. The problem is that you feel that the house is a mess all the time—and that's just not true.

Here the husband (H2) and the wife (W1) are both mind reading. Notice that the husband did not respond to the wife's mind-reading act by agreeing or disagreeing. Instead, he "retaliated" with a mind-reading act of his own.

W2: I don't think the house is always a mess, just sometimes it gets a little messy.

The wife responded to the husband's mind reading by telling him that his perception of her was wrong. It is better to give the other person feedback about the mind-reading assumption than to just ignore it as the husband did in H2.

H3: How can that be, when you want to spend all your time cleaning or complaining about cleaning?

W3: Don't keep on telling me what I think and how I spend my time—who do you think you are, Mr. Know-it-all?

Here the wife has told her husband that she doesn't like his mind-reading act.

H4: OK, you're right. Let's start this discussion all over again, all right?

W4: OK.

H5: Now, then, what do you feel is the problem with the house?

W5: I'm not happy with the way we have been dividing up the duties. In particular I feel that you do not help me clean. Is that true? How do you feel?

Now the couple is talking without mind reading—notice the difference between H1-W1 and H5-W5. The wife in W5 is telling her husband how she feels without asserting that it is a fact, as she did by mind reading in W1; she also checks it out with her husband.

Mind reading can also result in nondecisions where one person thinks one thing was decided, and the other thinks that another thing was decided.

Another term we put in quotes was "Kitchen Sinking." This term is borrowed from a book, *The Intimate Enemy* by Bach and Wyden, and is descriptive of a process that we, too, have observed in couples in the early stages of the SS Syndrome.

Kitchen Sinking
This term means that each discussion of *one* issue eventually winds up dragging in everything but the kitchen

sink. The discussion starts on one issue and, before there is a chance to explore that issue, one partner or the other drags in other gripes that may or may not be related. Pretty soon both people get the feeling that they have to deal with all of the issues at once, and the problem seems like a tangled knot, impossible to solve.

Middle Stages of the SS Syndrome

1. "Yes—butting."
2. Frustration reaches peaks.
3. "Cross-complaining."
4. Conversations end without resolutions.
5. Interruptions are frequent.

Yes—butting

In this act it seems like every attempt to make a suggestion or state a point of view to your spouse has something wrong with it. Your response to your spouse's suggestions or opinions, or your spouse's response to yours, is "Yes—but." The feeling you get is "I'm wrong again. Nothing I say is really acceptable." And the result is "What's the use of talking, anyway?" The person who says the *Yes—but* is often unaware of consistently rejecting his partner's views; he just feels that clarification is needed. The Yes—but is a frustrating habit that goes along with the SS Syndrome.

Cross-complaining

Cross-complaining occurs when each spouse states a complaint in response to a complaint. Below is an example:

W: I wanted to show you this sweater I bought on sale. It's just right, and I've been looking for it for a long time. But instead of being glad about it, you just got mad at me. That's not fair.

H: You've just got to learn to live within your means. I've wanted to take a nice vacation for a long time, but we can't afford it. And yet you don't go out and get a job to add to our income.

W: How can I feel like a woman when I can't even buy a simple white sweater I need?

Both husband and wife are thinking, "I'm not giving an inch. If only she (he) would just see my point of view and

12

how much it makes sense, then this fighting would stop."
Let's continue with this conversation.

H: I guess the major problem is we have enough money coming in for food, clothing, shelter and tuition, but we don't have enough to splurge on extras, and you have a tendency to spend money, without consulting me, on things you don't really need. Like that sweater you bought last week—that cost us $15 we didn't have.

W: Well, listen, you spend that much money every week on beer and cigarettes—so what if I treat myself to a present once in a while? You spend more than I do anyway.

H: That's not the point. You didn't consult me about the sweater and you have enough clothes to open a store.

W: That's not fair. We're talking about one lousy sweater compared to all the liquor you buy throughout the year.

The husband and wife are not responding to each other; rather, they are only summarizing their own complaints. This we call *Cross-complaining*. The pattern will continue until one or both spouses decide to focus on one complaint at a time and try to understand each other's point of view. Then they can contract to resolve the problems. How can the couple get out of the pattern? Let's see.

H: Well, I like to drink liquor and besides you drink some beer yourself. It's summer and we both like to have people over, and we serve them beer—that's why we have such a high liquor bill.

W: Oh, so it seems that you feel that you are justified in spending so much for liquor, and you also think I usually agree with spending money for beer.

The wife *edited out* her complaints. Instead, she decided to summarize her husband's position. Such a summary of the other's viewpoint will usually stop the Cross-complaining and help with problem solving. Let's go back to the conversation.

H: Yes, that's about it—I guess we do spend a lot of money on liquor and, as you say, I do drink most of it. I can understand your feeling that you deserve a little splurging on yourself once in a while.

13

The husband has summarized the wife, and they are ready to continue talking about the problem—rather than exchanging complaints. Without this summary of the other person, the Cross-complaining could continue as a negative exchange. A negative exchange involves a series of disagreements, put-downs, cross-complaints, or other verbal or nonverbal behavior that has a negative impact. It is a cycle of negative impact following negative impact, each person hurting the other and getting back for previous hurts.

Later Stages of the SS Syndrome

1. The "Standoff."
2. Escalating quarrels.
3. Heavy silences when together.

The Standoff

It is easy to recognize a Standoff when you see it in another couple, but very difficult to acknowledge in your own relationship.

The Standoff is a scenario which repeats itself in scene after scene. Although the vignettes differ in content, the basic structure is the same. Each partner stands firm in a position which is invested with a sense of right, of dignity, of pride. He says, "If only she would see all the stress that I'm going through and see all that I've done for her and for us—and if only she'd see how reasonable my position is, *then* we'd be OK." She has a similar attitude about her position.

And connected with "backing down" for each of them is a set of terrors, of *Catastrophic Expectations.* For example, she may think "If I give in, I will always be crawling to him, always in a secondary position." He may think "If I give in, then I'm just a henpecked husband, and I can't have that."

Who is right in a Standoff? They are usually both right. How do you end the Standoff? Someone must give, and the first two steps are (1) that someone must put himself in his partner's shoes and really try to see the world from another vantage point as well as the validity of that perspective; and (2) the Validation of that viewpoint must be communicated. The first step is hard enough. You'll be tempted to say, "Yes—but. . ." but you have to hold your tongue. Example:

W: Yes, I can see that he's been under a lot of job pressure and he probably thinks "Here I am, married to this bitch who doesn't support me through my failures, but just makes demands on me; well, I'm worn to a frazzle and I won't take any more gaff." I can see that from his perspective that that's valid. Yes—but . . . oh, I'll stop here.

H: I can see that she's got her own job worries and still has been taking care of the house and I've been irritable lately. She must feel that I've taken her for granted, that I treat her like a slave, that I keep complaining all the time and getting mad at her. But . . . oh, oh, I'm supposed to keep from "Yes—butting. . . ."

It's not enough to see the validity of your partner's perspective when *you* are the culprit. You must also be able *to communicate* that you see the validity of your partner's perspective. Ending the Standoff is not easy. Getting that message through is difficult, especially when you yourself feel hurt. What is the key to ending a Standoff? You must set aside those catastrophic expectations. When you think them, say to yourself, "I'm not going to let those consequences happen to me. For now, I've got to end this Standoff."

One of the most powerful things you can do is to first ask your spouse, *"What can we do to make things better?"* Second, when you are asked this question, try to answer it as specifically as possible. Your spouse will have an easier time responding to your suggestion if it is stated as clearly and specifically as possible.

If you are asked the question, "What can we do to make things better?" a good way to respond is, "Well, here's what I'd be willing to do to make things better."

We are asking you to suspend your evaluative attitude when trying these procedures. Tell yourself "I'll give these suggestions a try. I've really nothing to lose. Things I've tried in the past haven't worked too well, so I may as well see what happens if I follow these recommendations carefully." At first you may feel as though you're being very mechanical by asking your spouse "What can we do to make things better?" And if your spouse says this, you may think it is not really sincere, but is said only because of the program. You must be aware that it is often not easy to break old patterns for solving problems even though many of these old patterns are not successful at resolving conflict. So when you try to change the old patterns by using new skills, it may seem a little awkward. That's OK; in time you will learn how to incorporate the new skills into your own specific style for resolving problems and this new way of expressing yourself will soon begin to feel more natural.

To summarize, there are five things you've got to do to end the Standoff:

1. Genuinely try to see things from your partner's perspective. Don't "Yes—but." Summarize how you think your spouse feels.
2. Communicate that you feel your partner's perspective makes sense, is valid; even if you don't agree, you can *both* be right.
3. Be aware of the catastrophic expectations you are attaching to things. Tell yourself that you won't let these things happen.
4. Ask your spouse: "What can we do to make things better?"
5. State clearly and specifically what you will be willing to do to make things better. Present your recommendations in terms of a positive suggestion.

ENDING THE SS SYNDROME—
THE CHECK-OUT AND PARAPHRASE SKILL

How do you end the SS Syndrome? You start the Check-out and Paraphrase method. This skill involves several steps:

1. *Call a Stop Action:* All discussion stops and you talk about the discussion itself.

2. *Feedback:* Ask for feedback on your impacts. When giving feedback, make it clear, brief, specific, on topic. You are giving information to make things better, not resentments to get even.
3. *Listen to feedback:* What is the content? What is the feeling?
4. *Summarize and validate:* Paraphrase, in your own words, both content and feeling. Without *Validation,* this will be meaningless. You must get into your partner's shoes and see how reasonable it is for your spouse to feel this way. *And communicate this reasonableness.* This is very hard to do, especially when you yourself feel hurt or not listened to. But you *must* do it.
5. *Check Impact:* Check it with *Intent,* and discuss the discrepancy if one exists.

We cannot emphasize too greatly the importance of Validation. *Validation* means that you communicate to your spouse that, if you were seeing things his or her way, standing on his or her platform, with his or her assumptions about things, then *it would make sense and be reasonable to feel that way.* You are not saying "I agree with you," or "You're right, and I'm wrong." You are just admitting the possibility that another point of view may make sense, given some assumptions which you may not share with your spouse. Psychologists are used to the possibility that two seemingly different views or theories can both be right. There is a story about a wise old rabbi and his new assistant. The rabbi did marriage counseling, and one day he agreed to see a couple from his congregation while the new assistant watched attentively. First he saw the husband. The husband complained bitterly about his wife. The rabbi said "You know, you're right. It's terrible what you have to put up with." The man felt relieved, thanked the rabbi and left. Then the rabbi saw the wife. She complained bitterly about her husband. The rabbi said "You know, you're right. It's just terrible what you have to put up with." The woman felt relieved, thanked the rabbi and

17

left. The new assistant turned to the rabbi and asked, "But rabbi, how can they both be right?" The rabbi smiled at his assistant and said "You know, you're right too."

The point of the story is simply that for *Validation* you must assume, as a working hypothesis, that your spouse's views and feelings make sense if you can see them from his or her perspective. We cannot overemphasize the importance of genuine Validation (even in part). Summary *without* Validation will do nothing. In addition, Validation has a practical advantage. We have found that spouses often just want to feel that they have an important viewpoint, that what they say is important. By acknowledging an alternative viewpoint, your spouse will be more willing and pleased to work on a successful resolution of the problem.

If you have trouble with Validation, try saying to your spouse, "Look, can you help me to see this from your perspective? I'm having some trouble." If you are deadlocked on Validation, it may help if you take a break, take a walk by yourself, and get away from each other for a while. Schedule another time to talk. Validation is a hard thing to force. Once you are out walking, you may begin by griping to yourself about how terrible the things are that you have to put up with. Then you may forget about it for a while and just enjoy your walk. When you are more relaxed, you may find yourself thinking, "You know, he (she) isn't so dumb after all. Maybe there is some sense in his (her) feelings here."

Validation is hardest to do when you feel hurt, angry, sad, rejected, bitter, lonely, not understood, and it counts the most when it is hardest to do. When you finish this book, and get the most benefit from it, you will not stop feeling angry with your spouse. There will still be times when you hurt each other's feelings, when you communicate poorly, when you are in an SS Syndrome. When this happens, you should go into a Check-out and Paraphrase session.

18

Exercise 2   Be a Lousy Communicator

We'd like you to start learning about each of the symptoms of an SS Syndrome. Pick an "easy" issue after looking over the Problem Inventory in Appendix A (p. 178). If you have trouble finding an "easy" issue, think to yourself "Which event will come up in the next week that could be good, or that could wind up as a disaster?" For example, a dinner party, or going out to eat, or working together fixing the car, or a Sunday drive. Talk about this event. But first do it by being terrible, absolutely terrible communicators. Communicate in the worst way you can think of.

1. Don't listen
2. Mind read
3. Yes—but
4. Cross-complain
5. Drift off beam (drag in the "kitchen sink")
6. Interrupt
7. Do a Standoff
8. Heavy silence or escalate quarrels
9. Don't ever call a "Stop Action"
10. Insult each other
11. Don't validate, say "That's ridiculous. Now what I'm saying is . . . ."

Try doing this exercise when you will not be interrupted.

Exercise 3   Be a Good Communicator

When you've done Exercise 2 for a while, we'd like you to go back to *Check-out* and *Paraphrase.* Use the Floor and the Stop Action. This time, practice being a good communicator. You should:

1. Use Stop Action
2. Ask for feedback
3. Give good feedback
4. Listen to both content and feeling
5. Summarize and validate
6. Check Impact with Intent

Exercise 4   Troubleshooting Guide and Cassette Recorder

In this chapter you learned some new ways to solve problems. Once you know what a "Stop Action" is, you will find a cassette tape recorder a valuable aid for improving communication. Buy a recorder and some cassettes. Schedule a Family Meeting with your spouse to discuss an issue. Pick a time when you will just talk to each other without interruptions, and for *no other purpose* than to talk. Use "the Floor." Tape record your discussion. *After a Stop Action has been called, if you cannot decide which intervention to choose, do an instant replay of your discussion on the tape recorder to see if that will help.* This method is often effective for getting each of you to learn how you actually sound. Try to listen to the instant replay with the following questions in mind:

1. Where was I pigheaded?
2. Where was I not listening?
3. What was my spouse trying to say?
4. What was my spouse feeling?

Use the Checklist (p. 21) to rate *yourself.* Then use the Interim Troubleshooting Guide to find suggestions for improving communication (p. 24).

After you have called a Stop Action to discuss your Intent/Impact discrepancy, you can use the Checklist again to decide how things can be improved. This may help give focus to your discussion of the instant replay.

COUPLES AT-HOME CHECKLIST

Rate your own behavior by circling the number below that represents how well you did.

	Inadequate								Adequate
My listening	1	2	3	4	5	6	7	8	9
Sharing the Floor	1	2	3	4	5	6	7	8	9
My Intent/Impact match	1	2	3	4	5	6	7	8	9
Calling Stop Action when necessary	1	2	3	4	5	6	7	8	9
Validating my spouse's comments	1	2	3	4	5	6	7	8	9
Asking questions	1	2	3	4	5	6	7	8	9
Bringing the discussion back On Beam	1	2	3	4	5	6	7	8	9
Summarizing spouse	1	2	3	4	5	6	7	8	9
Using the Interim Troubleshooting Guide	1	2	3	4	5	6	7	8	9

After completing the Checklist, share your ratings with your spouse and use the Checklist to decide which skills from Chapter 1 you need to work on. It may stimulate discussion if you listen to the cassette recording of your conversation. Use the steps below.

1. Discuss the issue
2. As you discuss is there a time when *Intent* does not match *Impact*?
3. If so, call a Stop Action
4. Then use the Interim Troubleshooting Guide, the checklist, and do an instant replay of the last few minutes of your discussion.
5. Pick one way to improve the discussion.
6. Continue the discussion.

SELF-TEST

Answer these questions to see how well you have learned some of the basic concepts in Chapter 1. If you have trouble, re-read the chapter.

Review of Listening

1. Define good communication using "Intent" and "Impact."

2. When you have not communicated well, it is a good idea to call a _____ _____.

3. A basic problem in communication is the _____ _____ Syndrome.

4. Define this syndrome:

5. Define (in your own words):
   a. Off Beam:

   b. Mind reading:

   c. Kitchen Sinking:

   d. Yes—butting:

e. Cross-complaining:

f. The Standoff:

g. Validation:

6. How do you end the SS Syndrome?

7. Complete the following by noting the intervention you
   would use for each problem.

        Problem   *Intervention*

Not Listening

Off Beam

Cross-complaining

Standoff

Nondecisions

Negative Exchanges

Problem	Intervention
Not listening: You're not listening or you feel your spouse is not listening.	*Check-out and Paraphrase:* To build listening and speaking skills, you will use the following format:

a. Speaker speaks.
b. Speaker checks impact by asking listener to paraphrase his message.
c. Speaker corrects paraphrase by stating discrepancies between Intent and Impact.
d. Paraphrasing and Checking-out should focus on all three components of the message—content, effect, and relationship components.
e. Speaker and listener switch roles.
f. Process continues.

Off Beam:
The conversation keeps drifting off track.

Summarize and combine ideas of *both* spouses. Say: "I think we're getting off the track."

Cross-complaining:
Every time one spouse brings up what he or she feels is a reasonable issue, it is met by a more powerful counter complaint which short circuits any resolution of either issue.

Make an agenda:
List the complaints and deal with one complaint at a time, making sure to keep the conversation on beam. If a new complaint comes up, add it to the agenda, set a time limit on discussion with a new appointment to continue later. Try a cooling off period before discussing the complaints.

The Standoff:
In this game the spouse needs acceptance and approval so much

Validation:
Try honestly to see it from your spouse's point of view and com-

Problem

that every message includes the hidden message, "What about me and my feelings?" It is met by the same message from the other side, "Oh, yeah? Well, what about me?"

Another form of the Standoff is the "do-it-my-way-of-course" game in which neither spouse is willing to accept any other way of doing things than the obviously perfectly logical way he or she has already suggested a hundred times. Each spouse acts as if they are thinking "If only I can explain it once more to this thick-headed goon, he (she) will see the impeccable logic of my point of view. Now I know it won't work, but here goes patient, kindly old me again."

Nondecisions:
Decisions seem to get carried out without agreement by both spouses. One person thinks that one thing was decided, and the other thinks that another thing was decided.

Intervention

municate somehow that you can see how he (she) might feel that way and that it makes some good sense to feel that way. Accept some responsibility for how your spouse feels. *Then* try telling your side of it. Say something like, "I understand how you feel; I see your point of view and it makes sense to me." This is one form of reinforcing your spouse's point of view, which is one way of attempting to provide a partial positive instead of a complete negative during disagreement.

Give in, compromise. Experiment with some point of view. Try to see the other point of view, or at least find some good in it. And say so.

Ritualize the decision-making process:
Shake on it, write down what was decided, sign a contract, post the decision in a prominent place in the home.

25

Problem

Intervention

Negative exchange:
One spouse meets a painful re-
mark by producing one guaran-
teed to be equally (or more)
painful.

Break the cycle:
Talk about how you feel, and
try to take your partner's perspective no matter how hard
that may be at the moment. Try
it.

The positive exchange:
Look for those things you like
and make sure to follow a positive action with one you think
your partner will find positive.

2 LEVELING

In Chapters 2 and 3 you will learn two basic skills: **Leveling** and **Editing**. These two ideas were developed because we kept seeing two different types of couples. One type was caught in a dull relationship where their style was to avoid conflict and disagreement. A typical evening in the home of this kind of couple might begin:

H: (yawns) How was your day, dear?
W: (pleasantly) OK, how was yours?
H: Oh, you know, the usual.
W: Want a drink or dinner right away?
H: I don't know, whatever you want.
W: Anything special you want to do later?
H: I've got to go back to the office and do some work.

This couple may actually be carrying around a closetful of grievances that go unexpressed. One spouse may feel that it is a good marriage and may be totally surprised when suddenly, "out of nowhere," the other partner suggests divorce or separation.

The other type of couple is continually plagued by bickering, hassling, and constant arguing. It seems the only peace they ever get is when they are apart. Sometimes the bickering escalates out of control.

Both styles are painful but both can be changed. However, different remedies are needed to get both kinds of couples to communicate more effectively. For the con-

flict-avoiding couple, we suggest *leveling*. For the con-
flictual couple, we suggest *editing*.

We are not saying that it is always bad to avoid a
conflict, or always bad to fight. In fact, most couples we
see are a mixture of both extremes. Sometimes they get
into periods of avoiding conflict too much, and sometimes
they are at the other extreme of constant hassling. So it is
likely that you will benefit by both the leveling and the
editing skills.

Imagine yourself on a deserted island with a friend.
You have been on this island for several days, and it will be
a week before the boat returns to take you back to the
mainland. During the first couple of days you both were
having a good time swimming, lying in the sun, and eating
tropical fruit. As times goes on, however, you are getting
on each other's nerves more and more, and you begin to
wish the other person were somehow different, or perhaps
you wish you were with someone else. When you want to
eat, your friend wants to go swimming; when you want to
sleep, your friend becomes playful; and when you want to
read, your friend wants you to gather wood.

The more time you spend together, the more it becomes apparent that you are two very different kinds of
people. You each have different preferences, habits, and
tastes. At first, it seems that these differences are impossible boundaries to overcome and that you just may as well
try to ignore your disagreements, frustrations, and irrita-
tions, which are constantly increasing. You feel yourself
growing further apart from your friend, and yet you don't
know how to deal with your feelings. You think, "Well, in
a couple of days we will be off this island, and we'll never
have to talk to each other again"; or "Why bother to say
anything? There is no way we can get along happily together"; or perhaps, "This is what friendship is like. You
just can't be very close to another person." Whatever you
are thinking, each new episode illustrates the difficulties
you're having, and serves to strengthen the feelings of dis-
tance from your friend.

Take a moment now and imagine yourself on this island. Think of the beautiful blue water around you, of the lush tropical fruit, of the soft white sand, and also think of the tension you feel with your friend. Think of several days of low level conflict between you that neither of you has talked about, but that each of you knows is there. Try to make the scene as vivid as you can; close your eyes and picture yourself and your friend on this island. As you close your eyes, begin to think of ways to confront your friend with what is happening between you. Don't read on until you have thought of how the conversation might go when you talk about these issues.

It is probably not too difficult to see that, for some of us, marriage has become like the last couple of days on the island. We feel distant from our spouses, and the joy of spending time together that was once shared has been overcome by the problems that arise out of daily interactions together. Leveling will not miraculously produce intimacy between you, but it will begin a process of communication that will allow you to resolve conflicts in a productive way that can increase the closeness you feel for each other. Thus, we would like to suggest that, in close relationships, it is essential to let the other person know what your feelings and thoughts are if the relationship is to remain close.

Now suppose that the two people on the island knew they were going to have to work together for a long time, that they might have to plan for survival in the event of the ship's not returning. They would have to find some constructive method for working out their differences. We call this method "leveling," which is a way of not storing up, but rather of dealing with issues.

There are right and wrong ways to go about this communication task, and the rest of this chapter is designed to teach you, step by step, a method to level with your spouse. As you read this chapter, compare how you would have leveled with your friend on the island with the suggestions we outline for "constructive leveling."

HOW TO LEVEL

Leveling means that you tell your spouse what you are feeling by announcing your thoughts clearly and simply. It means that you should be transparent in communicating where you stand, and candid in signaling where you want to go. Some people are naturally good levelers, and they use this skill in all discussions and conflicts. For most of us, however, it is difficult at first to do a good job at leveling because it is easy to slip into stating what the *other person* is doing wrong, rather than stating what *you* are feeling.

Let's suppose you're in the car driving around town with your spouse. You feel your spouse is not being careful, and you are afraid you will become involved in an accident. You decide it's time to level your feelings. You might say "You're a rotten driver. You're going to get us both killed"; or you might be more tactful and say "Why are you driving so poorly today?" Neither of these messages conveys what *you yourself* are thinking and feeling. A better leveling statement would be "When I am in the car with you and you drive so fast, I feel scared." This statement makes your spouse *aware of you,* and does not hide your feelings in terms of what your spouse is doing.

It is also important to realize that each partner must learn how to *receive* a level message, as well as how to send one. If you were the driver in the car example above, you might get angry at your spouse for criticizing your driving. But you shouldn't. A good receiver responds by paraphrasing and validating what the speaker is saying. Thus, a good receiver might respond in the above example by saying "My driving is really making you nervous today. What can we do about that?"

Paraphrasing and Validation will allow the sender to see if his leveling is clear and specific, and will give him the opportunity to correct it. It will also demonstrate your willingness to understand your spouse's feelings.

Since leveling is difficult for most of us, we will spend the rest of this chapter outlining a method for constructive leveling. Keep in mind that the purpose of leveling is to make communication clear; to clear up what partners expect of each other; to clear up what is most agreeable and least agreeable; to clear up what is relevant and irrelevant; and to notice what things draw you closer together or push you further apart. Let's begin to look at methods for you to use when you want to level with your spouse; let's also consider how you can be a good receiver when your spouse levels with you.

How to Express Your Feelings

Catastrophic expectations. Many couples expect the consequences of expressing their feelings to result in catastrophe. Here are some possible catastrophic expectations:

1. My spouse will not love me anymore.
2. I will lose control of myself.
3. I will hurt our relationship *beyond repair.*
4. I will wreck everything.
5. It's not worth it to act that way.
6. I will seem like a weak person if I say what bothers me.

You've got to challenge the belief that it is absolutely necessary to be loved and approved of by your partner for *everything* you do. You can't please your spouse all of the time. There are occasions when you have to think of yourself, of your feelings, of what *you* need. And sometimes, if you have respect for yourself and your own needs, you will be easier to like and love. What people learn when they take advantage of you is simply that they can get away with pushing you around, that you will stand for it.

Behind these catastrophic expectations is the fear that expressing feelings means that you will lose all ability to decide when, to whom, under what circumstances, and how you express your feelings.

But remember, you are still you. No one is going to make you act in a strange or foreign way. When you experiment with change it will be in your own way, with your own style, at your own pace. You can experiment a little at a time to see how it works for you.

You must bear in mind, though, that all change involves doing some things differently. Therefore, new ways of acting or thinking may seem a bit stiff and phony at first. It is just like a new pair of shoes; new things share that in common. They have to be broken in, which means they have to fit *your* contours. You need to own them to make them personal, to make them *yours*.

How to Know What You Are Feeling

It takes practice to know what you are feeling. It involves getting to know your body and the signals it gives to tell you what you are feeling. It also involves becoming familiar with the typical pattern of thoughts that go along with specific feelings for you.

To help you start this process, use the sample feeling chart below. *When you want to know what you're feeling, look at the chart and select the word that best approximates how you feel at the moment.*

FEELING CHART

Positive

relaxed	secure	peaceful
calm	strong	confident
glowing	happy	interested
warm	busy	turned on
sexy	content	ambitious
excited	loving	imaginative
willing	bubbly	close-to-you

a little

I feel . . . somewhat

very

Negative

grouchy	alone	frustrated
sad	dumb	sorry
anxious	trapped	incompetent
tired	put down	rebellious
nervous	silly	confused
ashamed	shy	listless
bored	hurt	depressed
	guilty	restless

After you make your selection, make a note of the signals that that emotion has for you. Are you feeling anxious? Well, where does your body show it? Are there specific muscle groups that are tense—neck? Hands? Jaw? Chest? Gut? Is it hard to talk? Is your mouth dry? Are you sweating? Keep a diary of your own personal signs of emotions. Let your body teach you about yourself.

What were you thinking? Make a record of what you were thinking when you experienced each emotion. Then study your notes about your body and your thoughts. Eventually your signs of emotion should alert you to how you are feeling.

The Suggestion Box

Take two boxes (a cigar box will do) and label each box "Suggestion Box." One box is for you, and the other is for your spouse. If you want to start leveling but find it hard to do, put it down on paper and put it into your spouse's suggestion box. There are two rules. First, don't fish out a suggestion unless you think you are ready to listen to it, and want to hear how your spouse feels. Give yourself a bit of time to think over the note.

The second rule is: Schedule a time when the two of you can talk about the suggestion, a time when you can avoid being on the defensive. Also, don't forget what you learned in Chapter 1. The skills there (Summarizing and Validation) will help you to be a good receiver of level messages, and will help you to have a productive leveling discussion. Refer to the Interim Troubleshooting Guide (p. 24) during this discussion.

Be More Assertive

Initiating behaviors to get what you want in a situation. There are many situations in which you need to present a clear case about what you need, or about what you feel your rights are. To do this, you have got to think that what you want and need is important, that you are an important person, and that you are not going to let yourself be brushed aside easily.

33

Get yourself ready for these situations by thinking in your own mind that you are just as good as your partner, that this situation really matters to you, that it is worth taking a stand on. Then present your case succinctly, without attacking your partner. Try to get your spouse to see it from your point of view. State your goals in this situation, and restate them if necessary.

Asking people to do you a favor. You may find it hard to believe, but your spouse will like you better sometimes if he or she has had a chance to be of some help to you, especially if the efforts have *paid off.* So don't always think it is an awful imposition to ask your partner to do you a favor. The angel who is all giving and no taking is usually very resentful. Make things a two-way street. If this is difficult, ask your spouse to do you a favor today.

Requesting behavior change. The best way to ask your partner to change something is to be *specific* in your request, and try to state your request in terms of what you want the other person to do *more* of (not *less* of).

Another part of behavior change is picking a time and place for the discussion. Schedule a time for this meeting when neither of you has to rush off.

Finally, you will need to validate your partner's point of view of the situation; you may also have to accept modifications of your request. You will be most successful if you are willing to accept reciprocity in the change. And you will change, too.

Announce Your "Filter"
In Chapter 1 we discussed the speaker's and listener's filter, the one that operates to distort communication and functions to make the impact of a message different from the intention of that message. Sometimes we are unaware of which filter the listener or speaker may have in effect at a given moment, while at other times, with a little work, we have a good idea of which filter we may be using. The leveling process can be improved if you clearly state which

filter you feel is present as well as what the consequences of that filter are likely to be.

For example, if you had a difficult day at work and nothing seemed to go right, you might want to say to your spouse when you walk in the door, "Listen, I've had a lousy day at work today; everyone was getting on my back, and if I seem angry, it's not directed at you. It'd be best if you just left me alone for a while." By stating your feelings, your spouse does not have to guess what is going on with you, and you are less likely to become engaged in an argument which neither of you wants, but which begins because your filter distorts your intent. Recognizing and announcing your filter will also keep you from mistaking your spouse's intent. That is, because of your current filter, you may think your spouse is picking on you when in fact that is not the intention, and you yourself probably would not feel you were being unfairly accused had you not had such a bad day.

TOO MUCH LEVELING
Leveling does not mean that you should be unselective about *where, when,* or *how* you express your feelings. Honesty can be an excuse for striking back destructively. We'd like to teach you *how to level constructively.*

You ought to choose which issues are important to you and the time to level. Try a warm-up encounter within yourself to clarify in your own mind what is at stake. What do you predict would be the consequence of leveling on this issue at this time? An inner dialog can lead you to understand how you feel about the issue. Ask yourself the following questions:

1. Do I really have a legitimate bone to pick, or am I just in a rotten mood? Does it really have anything to do with my spouse? Maybe it's just my filter operating?
2. Is this an important issue? Am I overreacting to some trivial situation? Or is it worth discussing?
3. Do I simply want to air resentments? Am I really interested in solving anything?

4. How will my partner react? What price will I probably have to pay to win my point? What are the likely consequences?
5. Is this the right time for leveling, or can it be postponed with good effect?

The last question is important. If you are furious at your spouse and people are coming over for dinner in 20 minutes, you might really profit by leveling about having an issue to discuss, but also by scheduling a time to talk about it later in the evening. You are still leveling, but recognizing at the same time that you don't have to resolve everything immediately.

CONSTRUCTIVE AND DESTRUCTIVE LEVELING
Below are some examples of destructive, that is, non-problem solving ways of leveling and suggested alternatives.

Destructive Method 1   Character Assassination
Here you attribute bad or insulting characteristics or qualities to your spouse. For example, you can say "You are an insensitive person."

Constructive Alternative. Talk in terms of *action,* of what your spouse *does* that bothers you. For example, "You didn't ask me for *my* opinion on where to have dinner."

Destructive Method 2   Insults
Here you call your spouse a name that hurts his or her feelings. Examples: "You're a failure." "You're a slob."

Constructive Alternative. State specifically what your spouse does, in which specific situations, and how it makes you feel. Examples: "When you didn't ask for that raise today, I felt trapped by being poor." "When you don't wear a shirt at the dinner table, I feel that you don't think I'm special."

Destructive Method 3   Kitchen Sinking
Here you use complaints on many issues all at once to express your total exasperation. Example: "I'm fed up

36

with the house, with not going anywhere, with our sex life, and with our whole life style."

Constructive Alternative. Choose one important gripe and state it as follows:

> When you do X
> in situation Y
> I feel Z.

Be specific about X, Y, and Z. Example: "When you don't call me to tell me you're going to be late (X), when we have a dinner appointment (Y), I feel frustrated (Z)." This X, Y, Z formulation can help you to level constructively in all situations, and we suggest it as *the basic model* for constructive leveling.

Destructive Method 4   Cross-complaining
Here you do not use the listening and validation skills you learned in Chapter 1. Your leveling action then becomes a session in which you air resentments. In itself that may not be such a bad idea, but only if you listen to each other and validate complaints.

Constructive Alternative. Stick to one issue at a time.

Destructive Method 5   Complain constantly

Constructive Alternative. Choose an important topic to level about, and stick to that issue.

DESTRUCTIVE METHODS SUMMARIZED
Below is a list of the things you can do to be destructive in your leveling.

1. *Punish your spouse.* The implication is "You are bad," or "You are stupid," or "You are incompetent." These leveling statements usually have *shoulds* or *oughts* in them. Examples: "You should have . . ." or "What you ought to do is . . . ."
2. *Put your spouse down.* "You're a loser . . . ."
3. *Insult your spouse.* "You're a fat slob . . . ."

4. *Air old resentments.* "I can't ever feel good toward you because of what you did to me."
5. *Threaten your spouse.* "I feel that I don't want you to come home after work." Here you are threatening your spouse with ending the marriage.
6. *Be vague.* "You're driving funny today."
7. *Be general.* These statements usually begin with "You always" or "You never."

CONSTRUCTIVE METHODS SUMMARIZED
The constructive alternative is to level using statements like the following:

> When you do X
> in situation Y
> I feel Z.

You have to be as specific as you can about X, Y, and Z. Examples of constructive leveling are:

1. When you ask me for things in the morning, I get mad.
2. When you don't introduce me to people at a party, and don't spend time with me, I feel lonely and jealous.
3. When you criticize my driving, I feel like crying.
4. When you spend money that is not on our budget, I feel hurt and depressed.

All of these statements are leveling, and they specify the *action* (X), the *situation* (Y), and the *feeling* (Z).

WHEN TO LEVEL AND WHEN TO EDIT
At the beginning of this chapter we mentioned that we have seen two different types of couples. One type is constantly bickering and quarrels continually escalate, while the second type of couple avoids conflict at all costs. For the first couple, editing or politeness is most needed; for the second couple, leveling is what is called for. It is important to recognize that each couple, and each individual within a marriage, will have his or her own balance between leveling

and editing that is most comfortable. It is impossible to state the "perfect" balance between leveling and editing; all couples will differ on what is best for them. There are, however, guidelines to follow to help you decide what you need more of—more leveling or more editing. If you feel:

1. You are constantly in an argument with your spouse, or
2. You are more polite to a casual acquaintance than to your spouse, or
3. You are frequently insulting or putting your spouse down or wanting to have the last word in an argument

then editing at this point will likely be most useful for you.

If, on the other hand, you feel:

1. Very distant from your spouse and would like to be closer and more intimate, or
2. Unable to tell your spouse what you are thinking because you are afraid that you will not be able to resolve anything, or
3. Bored in the relationship

then leveling will be most useful to you now.

Try to evaluate the current status of your relationship in terms of leveling and editing, and come to some decision as to what you feel you yourself need more of, and what you believe the relationship needs more of. Once you have done this and Exercise 1, do Exercise 2 (p. 40).

SUMMARY

1. Leveling means that you are going to say how you feel.
2. It means that you are not going to store up grievances and let them all out at once.
3. You will begin to level using the suggestion box.
4. Leveling will mean that you are going to take the risk of being more assertive.

5. Leveling means picking your time to level, and the issue you will level about.
6. Leveling means saying, "When you do X, in situation Y, I feel Z" and being specific about X, Y, and Z.

Exercise 1   Discussing Issues

Schedule a meeting at home to discuss an issue. Precede your home meeting by having put at least one suggestion in your spouse's suggestion box, having read one intended for you, and having had a warm-up session with yourself. Spend part of the time on your suggestion and part on your spouse's.

Structure the meeting the way you learned in Chapter 1. Use the Floor and the positive and negative feedback cards. Have the Interim Troubleshooting Guide (p. 24) in front of you, and refer to it if you encounter difficulties.

Exercise 2   Leveling and Editing

This exercise is designed to allow you to begin discussing with your spouse the kind of balance between leveling and editing that you would like to achieve. Having thought about this issue alone, schedule a time together for a Family Meeting at which you will discuss the current balance between leveling and editing that exists in your marriage, and the optimal level that you each would like to achieve. Use the decision that you arrive at during this Family Meeting as your guide for "when to level and when to edit." Keep in mind that the next chapter on editing will give you a better idea of what is involved in editing and that you may want to have another discussion on the balance between leveling and editing once you have worked through the editing chapter.

SELF-TEST

Take this exam to see how well you learned the basic concepts in Chapter 2. If you find the test hard, go back and re-read the chapter.

1. Define leveling in your own words:

2. What are "catastrophic expectations"?

3. What are your own personal catastrophic expectations about leveling?

4. What is the Feeling Chart, and how do you use it?

5. How do you use the suggestion box?

6. What are the three aspects of being more assertive?

a.

b.

c.

7. Define "character assassination," which is one form of bad leveling.

8. What is the constructive alternative to character assassination?

9. What is the constructive alternative to insulting your spouse?

10. What is the constructive alternative to "kitchen sink-ing"?

11. Suppose someone tells you "I leveled with my spouse. I said 'You're insensitive. You never care about my feelings. I'm going to get a divorce if things don't change.' " What would you say to this person about leveling? What would be a better thing to say that is a better job of leveling?

12. Summarize leveling using an X Y Z statement.

_____ (X)

_____ (Y)

_____ (Z)

3 EDITING

Strange as it may seem, one of the first things to go in intimate relationships is the very courtesy and politeness that we are quite apt to continue to pay to total strangers. Dorothea Dix writes "It is an amazing but true thing that practically the only people who ever say mean, insulting, wounding things to us are those of our own households." You wouldn't think of interrupting a stranger to say "Good heavens, are you going to tell *that* old story again?" or snapping at someone at work if you are depressed. There is a kind of blindness that is easily adopted in marriage toward the feelings of spouses. Strangely enough, it is usually no one's fault since each spouse is likely to say "If she (he) would be more considerate of *my* feelings, well then I could be more considerate of her (his) feelings, but not until then." No one is willing to start being considerate all alone. And that is part of the purpose of this section on politeness. The goal of this chapter is to get both of you to take responsibility for courtesy and politeness at the same time, without waiting for the other person to act in a certain way first.

The most consistent research finding about what is different in the communication of strangers and people married to each other is that married people are ruder to each other than they are to strangers. They interrupt their spouses more, put their spouses down more, hurt each other's feelings more, and are less complimentary to each other.

While we have recommended constructive leveling to you in Chapter 2, we feel that leveling is most productive in a climate of mutual respect. And so we suggest that you be more polite to each other. We are really recommending some rules of etiquette that we and other researchers have observed in the interaction of mutually satisfied couples. It is also important to be polite at times when you are hurt or angry with each other but for some reason decide to postpone a leveling session.

We have seen mutually satisfying marriages that have little leveling and mostly politeness. We have also seen mutually satisfying marriages with little politeness and mostly leveling. That seems to be a decision of the couple's individual style. We would like you to learn how to level, and then to find your own personal balance between leveling and editing, a balance that is right for your style of living.

It is extremely important to regard your being polite in a situation as being independent of what your partner is doing. Politeness is something *you* decide to do. If both you and your spouse approach politeness this way, then what you do will not be latched to what your partner does, and there will be a greater chance of increasing politeness in your relationship. Thus, politeness will be a habit you will develop along with your spouse.

The worst thing you can do is to decide to stop being polite just because your partner has decided to be rude or impolite. When this happens, your discussions turn into impolite verbal battles, and both of you feel bad and unhappy. So, in order to avoid these negative interactions, *you must decide* to be polite at the same time your partner is being most unreasonable and impolite. This is when politeness really counts—and when it is most difficult. Of course, when your spouse is being polite, returning his or her politeness will produce pleasing, polite interaction, and both of you will feel good about your positive communication. Remember, you can always schedule a leveling session.

SUMMARY

Being polite is under your control; you decide whether to be polite or impolite. The basic message of this unit so far is that *your decision to be polite must not be latched to the way your spouse is acting.* Rather, you decide to be polite because you care about your spouse and your relationship.

The next section will provide you with some easy hints on how to be polite in an intimate relationship.

NINE RULES OF POLITENESS

Below are nine rules that we have found helpful. What is the basic idea behind being polite? It means doing a bit of mental work called "editing" in which you decide between several things to say and do, and picking the one that is most polite. Below are some guidelines to help you learn how to become a good "editor." Remember that these are rules for the times when you are *not* leveling.

The Don'ts of Politeness	*The Do's of Politeness*
1. Don't say what you can't do, or what you don't want to do.	Say what you *can* do and what you *want* to do.
2. Don't complain or nag.	Give sincere and positive appreciation. If you have an issue to resolve, schedule a leveling session.
3. Don't be selfish.	Be courteous and considerate.
4. Don't hog the conversation.	Express interest in your spouse's activities; try to listen; ask questions.
5. Don't suddenly interrupt.	Give your spouse a chance to finish speaking.
6. Don't put your spouse down.	Say things that you honestly feel and that you think your spouse will like.
7. Don't put yourself down.	Criticize your ideas, not yourself.
8. Don't bring up old resentments.	Focus on the present situation. If you have an issue, schedule a leveling session.

| 9. Don't think only of your own needs and desires. | Think of your spouse's needs and desires; be empathic. If you have an issue to resolve, schedule a leveling session. |

The nine rules are given below with examples and explanations.

Say What You Can Do and What You Want to Do

Suppose your spouse asks you if you have time to go shopping for something for your home that you both feel you need to buy. You say to yourself "I've got a million things to do today, and only two hours free time between three and five."

You can tell your spouse what you cannot do: "I've just got a million things to do. I've got to do _____ and I've got to do _____" and so on. Or you can say "I've got two hours free when I can go shopping, but only from three to five."

In this example you edited what you decided to say, and picked the statement that explained what you could do rather than what you could not do. Here is another situation. Write in a polite response in the space provided.

You are discussing with your spouse how to spend your summer vacation. Your spouse says he (she) wants to take a long trip. You say to yourself, "That would take too much time and cost too much money; I only have one week of vacation." You say (write your answer in the space below):

One polite response is: "How about going camping or some place closer? That would take less time, and we could do it within the week I have off from work."

In this response you successfully edited the *can't* statement and decided to replace it with a statement telling your spouse what you can do on your vacation.

Give Sincere and Positive Appreciation

Breakfast is served, and you notice that the eggs are over-cooked. That annoys you. However, the orange juice is hand squeezed. You like that. Your spouse says "Well, what do you think of your breakfast?" You can be impolite and say "Oh, boy, rubber eggs again." Or you can be polite and say "I just love orange juice this way. Thanks for taking the time to hand squeeze the juice."

Again you have edited out what you were going to say and decided to give an honest appreciation instead of a complaint. It's your choice. It's in your power to decide whether to be polite or to complain. If cooking is an important issue, remember that you can always decide to discuss this issue and level about it.

Here is another situation; write in a polite response in the space provided.

Your spouse bought a present for your birthday which you really have no use for. You say to yourself "What the hell am I going to do with this? I wish I'd gotten something I like." You say:

One polite response is: "Thanks for the birthday present; it was nice of you to remember." Here you have *edited* out the negative complaint and have focused on the positive aspects of the situation. Again, remember that if this is an important, *constant* issue, you can ask for a meeting to discuss it and to level.

Compliments that are actually insults. Be careful to avoid giving a compliment that includes a resentment. For example, if your spouse has just finished painting the kitchen and has done a good job, a poor compliment would be: "Well, it's nice to see that you've finally done *something* right." You'd be mad if your spouse said that to you. So take care not to tack on an insult to the compliments you pay.

Example: Your spouse is finally ready to go out and you say "Ready at last. It's about time." That is a poor compliment. You might just say "Hey, you look good," or "That was worth waiting for. You look nice."

Be Courteous and Considerate

You are tired and would prefer not to be bothered. Your spouse comes into the room and says "Would you mind doing the dishes tonight? I'm frazzled." You know your spouse is tired, but so are you. Yet this is not a terribly unreasonable request, just a bit annoying. You can say "Look, what about *me*? I'm tired, too. *You* do the dishes tonight. I'm resting." Or you can be courteous, which may mean deciding to do the dishes and saying "OK, I'm tired, but I wouldn't mind doing them tonight. You look bushed."

Again you have edited what you were going to say and decided to be courteous and considerate.

Here is another situation; write a polite response in the space provided.

You and your spouse are on a trip, and he (she) has been trying to help you with the directions as you drive. It's gotten to the point where the suggestions are beginning to bother you. You say:

A polite response is: "I know you're trying to help by giving me directions, honey, but I'm getting confused. Perhaps we should pull over and decide how to get there." Here you are recognizing your spouse's positive intent as well as communicating your discomfort in a considerate and courteous manner. Another polite response is to say to yourself "Gee, I know he (she) is trying to help, and it's not really bothering me that much. I'll let it slide." Here you decided *to edit* all the negative statements; you are being considerate by not saying anything.

Express Interest In Your Spouse's Activities; Be A Good Listener

At the end of the day you and your spouse may share the events of the day. Again, you can express interest by asking questions about your spouse's day, or you can hog the conversation, keep talking about your day, and expect rapt attention.

You can edit what you say by deciding not to talk about yourself and instead trying to find out about your spouse, getting your spouse to talk, asking questions, being attentive, showing that you are listening. Here is another situation; write a polite response in the space provided.

You get home from work and turn on the TV to watch the news. Your spouse comes into the room and mentions that he (she) had an interesting day. You say:

A polite response is: "Tell me about your day," or "And what was so interesting about today?" instead of (1) ignoring your spouse and watching TV or (2) hogging the conversation and complaining "I had another boring day at work." Here successful editing involves (1) scanning your mind, searching for a message which shows you are interested in your spouse, and (2) deciding not to hog the conversation by speaking only about yourself.

Give Your Spouse a Chance to Finish Talking

You and your spouse are discussing an interesting topic. While she (he) is talking, you think of a great idea you really want to express. You can interrupt in the middle of a sentence and rudely insert your opinion, or you can be polite and ask her (him) "Are you finished?" before you start speaking.

Here you are editing your desire to interrupt your spouse, and you are giving her (him) a chance to continue speaking. Here's another situation; write the polite response in the space provided.

It's after dinner and you're in the living room. Your spouse is telling you about his (her) day. You remember that you have to make a very important phone call. You say:

A polite response is: "Excuse me for a moment, honey. I just remembered I have to make a very important phone call. Then I want you to continue telling me about your day." Here you have accomplished two very important things: (1) You have done your editing work and have found a polite way to interrupt your spouse, and (2) you have communicated the message to your spouse, "I've been listening to you and I am interested in what you're saying." Remember, leveling sessions can be scheduled for issues.

Say Things You Think Your Spouse Will Like
In order to help you out, your spouse has taken the car to the gas station to get it repaired. However, the serviceman was not told exactly what was wrong with the car and now you have to spend more money on further repairs. You can put your spouse down by saying "Boy, that was dumb," or you can be polite and say "It was nice of you to help me out when I was so busy."

Here you have successfully edited the "put down" and have focused on the positive side of the situation. You have decided to say something you think your spouse will like (that is, "You're a nice person").

Suppose you are trying to say something nice to your spouse. You scan your mind for nice things to say. Again, you can *edit* the nice things so that you say that one thing you know your spouse is *most* likely to appreciate. Remember, say and do something that you think your spouse would most appreciate. Just as you might ask yourself "What is her (his) favorite color?" when buying a present; ask yourself "What is important to him (her)?" when editing all the nice things you could say.

Here is a situation; write a polite response in the space provided.

Your spouse has been really nice to you the last few days, and you say to yourself "What can I say that she (he) will really like to hear?" You say:

If you can't think of anything nice to say, then ask your spouse what she (he) would like to hear from you. This can be done by saying "What do you wish I'd say to you?" or "What do I say that makes you feel good?" Similarly, you can help your spouse to be polite by giving feedback about the things that make you feel good.

Criticize Your Ideas, Not Yourself
You have had a fight and you realize that you were wrong. You say to yourself "How can I say that I was wrong?" You can say "I'm a rotten person; why do I always say stupid things"; or you can say "I was wrong for saying that. I'm sorry—what can I do to make things better?"

Here you have edited a self put-down; instead you have decided to accept responsibility for what you did. Also, you are asking your spouse to tell you what you can do to help resolve the situation.

Why is it impolite to put yourself down during conversations with your spouse? Because it puts your spouse (who is trying to be polite) on the spot to either build you up or say something to support you. So don't put yourself down. It is, however, important to admit that you are wrong when you are wrong. There's nothing impolite about that. You can say "I was wrong," or "I'm sorry I said that," or "That was a dumb thing to do," or "That wasn't a very good idea." In that way you are putting down your ideas and actions, but you are not saying that you are a valueless person. It is an insult to someone who loves you to say that they are dumb enough to love a worthless person. So, if you must say something negative to admit that you were wrong, *edit those statements so that you do not put yourself down.* If you want support or your ego bolstered, why not just say that you're feeling low and in need of support at the moment? You will probably get support by asking for it directly more often than by putting yourself down.

Here's another situation; write the polite response in the space provided.

After telling your spouse for days that you are sure he (she) has overdrawn the checking account, the bank statement arrives and there are no problems with the balance. Your spouse comes into the living room after you realize your error, and you say:

A polite response is: "I'm sorry I accused you of overdrawing the account; it was unfair of me to do that before seeing the bank statement." Here you have successfully edited your message by deciding to accept responsibility for your actions without impolitely putting yourself down.

54

Focus on the Present Situation

You are upset because your spouse didn't pay attention to you at last night's party. You can say to her (him) "This is the last straw; you drink too much at parties and you spend too much money on clothes. This stuff has got to stop," or you can edit out "old business," and talk about the current situation in a polite way.

It is impolite to dig up past events to throw at your spouse during discussions. Taking a discussion back into the past can only serve to increase the current problem. This rule also holds for situations when you are discussing one issue, and you bring up other issues and complaints. These "unloading sessions" tend to occur when you don't communicate about problems as they arise.

Here's another situation; write down the polite response in the space provided.

You have been mad at your spouse for the past few days. Dinner has been unpleasant, the house has been a mess, and finally today he (she) forgot to pick up the car at the gas station. You come home after running an errand your spouse should have done. You say:

A polite response is: "You must have been pretty busy today; you forgot to pick up the car at the gas station." Here you are editing the old business of the messy house and late dinner and focusing on the present situation, the car. Also, you are being polite by suggesting that your spouse is busy. This response is a good example of being polite when your spouse is not being polite. Remember, politeness is most important when it is most difficult.

Requests that are actually complaints. If you want something, don't throw in a complaint with your request. That

55

just sours things. If you want to go out for dinner, and you say "Why don't we get dressed up and go out for dinner? I'm tired of how you've looked at dinner lately," you are just inviting a fight.

Example: "Why aren't you kinder to me? If you knew how difficult it was to live with you, you'd feel sorry for me and be nicer to me." (Leave out the complaint and make your request specific.)

Think of Your Spouse's Needs and Desires
Be Empathic

This last rule sums up all of the previous ones. When you notice yourself thinking only of yourself, edit those thoughts and decide to think about what your spouse needs and wants. In a relationship where politeness reigns, both spouses' needs and wants are being met because you are both thinking of yourselves. However, remember that you must decide to be polite, *independent* of your spouse's actions.

For instance, you want to go out in the evening. You say to yourself "I wonder if he (she) wants to go. I bet not. What would be fun to do together, something we'd both enjoy?" You say "What would be fun to do together? What mood are you in? I'd like to go out."

Here you are thinking of your spouse's feelings. Such behavior is catching, and positive rewarding interactions can be expected to increase the more you and your spouse share politeness in your relationship through successful editing.

SUMMARY

1. Say what you *can* do and what you *want* to do.
2. Give sincere and positive appreciations.
3. Be courteous and considerate.
4. Express interest in your spouse's activities; try to listen; ask questions.
5. Give your spouse a chance to finish speaking.
6. Say things that you honestly feel and that you think your spouse will like.

7. Criticize your ideas, not yourself.

8. Focus on the present situation.

9. Think of your spouse's needs and desires; be empathic.

If you have trouble with these nine rules, and quarrels still continue to escalate without relief, read Chapter 7 "Getting Through a Crisis." There are some suggestions about rules of etiquette in the home that couples we've seen have found helpful to create a much more pleasant working relationship.

To summarize, we are suggesting in this chapter that leveling sessions be scheduled to work on issues, but that leveling take place in a climate of positiveness, politeness, and consideration for one another.

Exercise 1   Getting In Touch

We want you to pretend for just one week that one of you is a long-lost friend and lover you haven't seen in a few years who is visiting your home. One of you take the role of host, and the other be the guest. During this week, try to be as kind and polite as a guest would be to a host and a host would be to a guest. Schedule some time (say half an hour) each day just to talk and catch up with one another. You may know a lot about what your spouse is doing, but how much do you know about what she (he) is thinking and feeling? What are your spouse's worries, hopes, joys, dreams, terrors, wishes? We'd like you to get in touch with your spouse this week, as you would with a friend.

Try not to be defensive when your spouse finally tells you her (his) thoughts and feelings. Just listen, and try to understand. If you have trouble with this, read Chapter 8, "Making a Good Thing Better," which includes suggestions for improving conversations.

During this week we'd also like you to plan and go out on a date, just the two of you. If there are issues between you that would make this hard, schedule a leveling session to clear the air before you go.

Exercise 2   Editing

Test your knowledge of the nine rules of editing. Pretend

that these are real situations; write in what you might actually be *most* likely to say in each situation. Don't write in what you think you *ought* to say, but what you actually might say if you were to use good editing.

1. It's Saturday and your spouse has asked you if you have time to go shopping for something you both feel you need for the house. You say to youself "Wow—I have so much to do today; the only free time I have is between three and five." You say:

2. Breakfast is served, and you notice that the eggs are overcooked. That annoys you. However, the orange juice is hand squeezed. You like that. Your spouse says "Well, what do you think of breakfast?" You say:

3. Your spouse comes over to you after dinner and says "Would you mind doing some of my chores tonight? I'm just dog tired." You say to yourself "I'm pretty worn out tonight, and I want to be left alone." You say:

4. You and your spouse finally get a chance to sit down and talk after a full day. You say to yourself "I've got a whole lot to say. I hope he (she) wants to listen." You say:

5. You and your spouse are discussing an interesting topic. While your partner is talking, you think of a great idea and really want to express it. You say:

6. In order to help you out, your spouse takes the car to the gas station to get it repaired. However, the serviceman was not told exactly what was wrong with the car, and now you have to spend more money on further repairs. You say:

7. You have had a fight with your spouse, and you realize that you were wrong. You say to yourself "How can I say that I was wrong?" You say:

8. You are upset because your spouse didn't pay any attention to you at last night's party. You say to yourself "This is the last straw. This, on top of all the other things that have gone wrong, is too much! Boy, am I getting mad!" As you are driving home, you say:

9. You want to go out tonight; however, you know that your spouse really doesn't feel like going out. You say:

4 NEGOTIATING AGREEMENTS

In this chapter we will examine other ways you can *change your behaviors* to improve your marital relationship. You must keep in mind that if you want things to change in your relationship, *you also* will have to change. "Change" for many people is rarely an easy process or one that occurs overnight. Yet it is our human potential for change that provides the necessary conditions for working out satisfying relationships with friends, family, and lovers. Everyone can change if they want to. Before reading on, turn to Exercise 1 (p. 71) on self-change.

In thinking about change, we will speak in terms of *increasing the frequency of positive behaviors.* This is an important point since most of us have a tendency to state our dissatisfactions with our spouses as a complaint which requests stopping some behavior. "I want you to stop nagging me about a raise," rather than the positive suggestion, "I would like you to pay me more compliments about my work."

Since we have this tendency to state complaints as a command to others to reduce the frequency of certain behaviors, it is not easy for us to clearly state in a specific way the behavior we want increased. One of the major goals of this unit is to help you make specific complaints to your spouse. Once you are able to make specific complaints, it becomes possible to take the important next step which turns the specific negative complaint into a specific positive recommendation for dealing with a gripe.

61

THE FAMILY MEETING
BEGINNING TO WORK IT OUT

We have found it useful for couples working in this phase of the program to set up a meeting time once or twice a week to talk over how each feels about the relationship. During this time you can talk over anything that is bothering you, things you are angry about, or simply share with each other both the good and bad feelings you are currently experiencing. The Family Meeting will be a key time for you to put into practice all the specific communication skills you have already learned. A Family Meeting that is carried through with good communication will be a very satisfying experience for both of you as you will see if you carefully follow the steps outlined below.

When you sit down to resolve a problem at a Family Meeting, it will help if you think of the meeting in terms of three distinct stages:

1. Gripe time
2. Agenda building
3. Problem solving

GRIPE TIME

The first stage of a Family Meeting is the time when gripes and resentments can be vented. During this stage it is important for you to realize that your spouse's gripes are not necessarily true or false and it is not, repeat *not,* your job to defend yourself. Your job during the gripe time is to listen to your spouse's gripes, and to make sure that you understand what your spouse is saying. Remember that resentments and gripes are always one person's way of seeing a situation. So they are always right. Even if you don't agree with the details, a gripe expressed to you is a feeling your partner has. Below is a summary of what you should and should not do during gripe time.

Do's	*Don'ts*
1. Do state clearly and specifically the gripes you have about your spouse.	Don't try to defend yourself by showing that your spouse is wrong.

2. Do follow the rules for constructive leveling when you gripe.	Don't sulk and withdraw.
3. Do listen and accept your spouse's gripes as legitimate feelings.	Don't meet your spouse's gripe with a gripe of your own. Don't cross-complain. Don't assume you know what your spouse means; make *sure* you know.

Since Number 1 under "Do" is important, let's spend some time on exactly how we can transform a *negative nebulous* complaint, such as "You're a failure," into a *specific negative* complaint, such as "It bothered me that you didn't ask your boss for a raise; it made me feel trapped." This style of presenting your gripes will make *problem solving* an easier task for both of you.

An example of a *negative nebulous* gripe might be "You never pay any attention to me." When turning the negative nebulous into a specific gripe, it is useful to think of a specific instance that would give rise to your gripe. Thus, the above gripe can be made specific: "When you come home at 5:30, you never ask me any questions about how I've spent *my* day. You usually just tell me about your day."

Now when you and your spouse are in "gripe time," and exchanging gripes, you will have *to help each other* to make gripes specific. When you help your spouse make a gripe specific, ask the following questions:

1. What specifically do I do or not do that bothers you?
2. In what situations does this occur?
3. Can you give me an example of once when it happened? (If not, you can ask, "Well, the next time it happens, point it out, OK?")

Here is an example of a gripe time conversation:

H: The house is always a mess, and I can't stand it.
W: The whole house isn't always a mess.
H: It usually is.
W: What specifically bothers you?

H: I guess the kitchen bothers me most; I hate that room.

W: Why?

H: It bothers me that the dishes pile up for days instead of being done right away. It's depressing.

W: You're saying you want to get the dishes washed soon after meals?

H: Yeah, I hate to see the kitchen a mess.

W: Well, if we both didn't have to go out so much in the evening, they would get done.

H: The dishes ought to be done right after every meal. We'd have time for that.

W: We probably would if you'd lend a hand. That's a problem.

H: So you're saying I don't do enough after meals to help clean up.

W: That's right, and that bothers me.

H: Well, I do a lot of the cooking so I thought you should clean up.

W: You may do the cooking, but I do the shopping and I would like some help with that.

AGENDA BUILDING

After all the immediate gripes are aired by both you and your spouse, it is time to make a list of the specific issues you will try to resolve. You may not be able to solve all the gripes that have been brought up; therefore, you should pick those things that are most important to you right now. It is probably best *to limit yourself to one major gripe.* In this stage of the Family Meeting you are building an agenda for the remainder of the meeting. Your job in the agenda building stage is summarized below.

Do's	*Don'ts*
Do pick one or two gripes that you will work on in the Family Meeting.	Don't throw in a new gripe every time one comes to mind.

Let's continue the above conversation as it moves into the agenda building stage.

H: OK. We've got a lot on the table. I want a clean kitchen, and you want me to help with the dishes after meals?

W: Right.

H: Do you want to work on how we can keep the kitchen clean and hold off on who is doing more by going shopping or doing the cooking?

64

W: Well, I really feel I do more by going shopping than you do by cooking. Besides, I sometimes do the cooking and you never do the shopping.

H: We can't work on all these issues; can we decide on one to solve right now?

W: You're right. I guess I threw in another gripe. OK, I guess we should work on keeping the kitchen clean because that bothers you most, too.

PROBLEM SOLVING

In the gripe time stage you and your spouse have helped each other to turn negative nebulous gripes into specific negative gripes. During agenda building you have decided on one or two important things you will work on in this meeting, and your spouse will have done the same. In the problem-solving stage, you will go a step further and turn the specific negative gripes that are identified as important into *specific positive suggestions* that will remedy the specific problem. The positive suggestions will always be in the form of a recommendation for *increasing the frequency of a positive behavior* that answers the gripe. Here is an example illustrating the steps to follow in turning a negative gripe into a positive suggestion.

Gripe Time:

The negative nebulous   "You don't respect me."

The specific negative complaint   "At the party last night, when everybody was suggesting which movie was the best in town, you laughed at me when I said *Gone with the Wind.*"

Problem Solving:

The specific positive suggestion: "When I say something in a group, show that you are interested in it because it's my opinion. You can do this by saying something like, 'Yeah, Sally really did like *Gone with the Wind.* I remember that.'"

65

Many couples never go on to the problem-solving stage when they discuss a problem. The conversation ends after agenda building. In the conversation above, the husband might add: "Good, I am glad we agreed to keep the kitchen clean. Let's go watch TV." The question remains: How will they keep the kitchen clean now that they have decided to do so? Let's follow the conversation as it moves through the problem-solving stage of the Family Meeting.

H: Oh, good. How about if I do the cooking, and you do the cleaning up? And if you help me cook, I'll help you clean. And if you cook, I'll do the cleaning.

W: That sounds good. I'd also like to go out to eat on Tuesday and Thursday when we both have our busiest days.

H: Great idea! We can easily afford to eat out twice a week.

W: So whoever cooks, the other person cleans up, and if we both cook, we'll split the cleaning. And on Tuesday and Thursday we'll eat out.

H: OK—let's shake on the deal!

In order to specify which behaviors will be increased in problem solving, and exactly what the consequences of increasing these behaviors will be, we must discuss how to form *a contract.* Forming the contract will be the last step involved in working on each gripe. The goal of the contract is (1) to identify clearly the behaviors that will be changed so that you and your spouse can evaluate how well you kept your end of the bargain, and (2) to provide an incentive for increasing the frequency of positive behaviors.

In the contract you will agree to increase the frequency of a specific positive behavior that will remedy your spouse's complaint. Likewise, your spouse will agree to increase the frequency of a specific positive behavior that will remedy your specific positive complaint. You will also both agree on appropriate rewards you will each receive if you live up to the contract!

The rewards you select should not place a burden on your spouse. Here is an example of a contract worked out by a couple.

NEGOTIATION FORM

Husband

Behavior to be accelerated:	*Reward:*
I will help clean up the dishes after meals when I don't do all the cooking. I will go out to eat on Tuesday and Thursday.	Spouse will go bowling with me on Saturday.

Wife

I won't leave my clothes out in the bathroom, but will hang them in the closet.	I will be able to buy the blouse I've been wanting.

Let's take a moment now and review the guidelines for making a daily meeting with your spouse productive. There are two basic rules to follow:

1. *Accept responsibility* for your actions instead of blaming your spouse. You do have a choice about what you will do or say at the moment.
2. *Be specific* and express yourself clearly.

Overall, what you want to do in a Family Meeting is to be able to move from feeling angry and hurt to being able to express yourself clearly and negotiating an agreement to accelerate positive behaviors.

When you start a meeting, you may feel angry or hurt or just like running away. First, you need to set aside a time just for griping, a time when you and your spouse can vent your resentments. During *gripe time* it is not necessary for you to answer your spouse's resentments. Just vent them specifically and see that things do not escalate. If you feel the conversation escalating and can't seem to do anything about it, take a ten-minute break.

Next, you will *build an agenda*. From your resentment list select one, or at the most two, important things you will work on in this meeting; give your spouse a chance to do the same.

The next thing is *problem solving*. You have to move from specific negative gripes to positive suggestions for increasing the frequency of positive behaviors.

To summarize, the Family Meeting should proceed as follows:

Stage	Your Job
Gripe Time	1. State clearly the gripes you have about your spouse.
	2. Follow the rules for constructive leveling.
	3. Listen and accept your spouse's gripes as legitimate feelings.
	4. Work to understand your spouse's gripes by summarizing and paraphrasing what was just said.
	5. Help your spouse to turn negative nebulous gripes into specific negative gripes.
Agenda Building	Decide on one or *at most* two gripes you feel are the most important to work on right now in the problem-solving stage. (Your spouse will do the same.)
Problem Solving	1. Together with your spouse, turn the specific negative gripes (chosen in the agenda building) into positive suggestions for increasing the frequency of a positive behavior that will answer the gripe.
	2. Form a contract in which you both agree to increase a positive behavior. Determine the reward you will get for increasing your behaviors.

In Chapters 1, 2, and 3 you learned important skills that provide the basic framework for successful problem resolution. However, while you may have been able to accurately label issues, without this section you might not be able to solve them. Hopefully, in this chapter you will learn to come to a solution both of you will be pleased with. In this chapter all of the previous skills come into play. At gripe time, feedback and validation play an important role in understanding your spouse's gripe and communicating your own gripe. Unless there is an honest effort to clearly understand the problem issues, the final resolution will be inaccurate and more than likely will have to be repeated again in the future. Notice that in making a gripe specific the leveling guideline is useful:

When you do X
In situation Y
I feel Z

We simply go one step further at this point and have you phrase the "I feel Z" as a specific positive suggestion.

RESISTANCE TO CHANGE

When discussing the Standoff, we mentioned that some couples have developed ineffective patterns for dealing with conflict or disagreement. In these relationships, partners try to reach decisions, but the conflict is only temporarily reduced and disagreements are not resolved. Since these patterns are temporarily rewarding, the same pattern is repeated many times. It is this repetitive pattern of interaction that has been called a *marital game* because it seems to have rules, as if both people were playing by agreed-upon guidelines. Many couples appear to be stuck in these not-so-good games simply because the problem is not resolved and is therefore likely to recur in similar form.

It is these not-so-good games that often block couples from achieving honest communication, and from successfully resolving conflict through negotiated agreements. The following material is intended to suggest that for each not-so-good game you learn to recognize that there is a good game you can put in its place. The list below includes some common not-so-good games we have found to occur frequently along with its suggested opposite good game. You will notice that many of the good games have been presented in the contracting sections. Our purpose here is to emphasize that couples experiencing difficulty working through conflicts and disagreements are often falling into the pitfalls of the old games, and that they must work to recognize this and substitute a good game in place of the old patterns.

COMMON MARITAL GAMES

Not so good

1. *The mind reading act:* Spouses express the attitude, "My partner should know what I want, and if I have to tell him (her), then it's no good."

2. *Character assassination:* Spouses express a wish for partner change as a *nebulous* wish for a change in character or personality. (For example, "I wish you were less passive," or "I wish you were more sensitive.")

3. *The complaining rut:* Spouses seem to be unable or unwilling to describe the changes they want in their partners in terms of increasing positive behaviors; wishes for change are expressed in terms of decreasing negative behaviors.

Good

Express yourself: Tell your partner as clearly as humanly possible what you want, what you think, and what you feel. Follow the rules for good leveling.

Be specific: Express wishes as a *specific* request for a *specific* change in action in *specific* situations.

Pinpoint the positive: Express wishes for change in terms of *positive actions* you would like to see *more* of (acceleration of the positive).

SUMMARY

1. Express yourself clearly (do not expect your spouse to read your mind).
2. Be specific.
3. Pinpoint the positive (express change in terms of accelerating the frequency of positive behaviors).

SELF-CHANGE: LEARNING TO PINPOINT THE SPECIFIC POSITIVE IN YOUR OWN BEHAVIOR

We stated earlier that if *you want* things *to change* in your relationship, *you* will have to change. You may be saying to yourself right now "I don't have to change; if my spouse changed, everything would be OK. It's not me that's the problem. No way!" It's OK to think this. We only ask that you try our suggestions and give them a fair chance. After you try them, you will then be able to evaluate them to see if they are useful to you. But it is not possible to evaluate the tasks we are asking you to do *before* you give them a try, so *suspend evaluation* for the time being!

Your first "behavior change" assignment involves two parts. In Part I you will count the frequency of a behavior of yours which you would like *to increase* in frequency. For example, the behavior may be to pay your spouse compliments, or to complete errands, or do chores around the house. Take a moment now and decide which behavior you would like to increase.

Exercise 1   Self-Change

If you are having trouble deciding on a behavior, perhaps the following questions will help you assess your own resources.

1. List three of your most important strengths.
   a.
   b.
   c.
2. List three aspects of your behavior which you would like to change.
   a.
   b.
   c.

Based on either your strengths or the self-identified behaviors you want to change, select a behavior you will increase.

At this point you have selected a behavior you will increase. Please write this behavior in the space provided.

Behavior I will increase is: _____

In Part I of this exercise you are to count the frequency of your chosen behavior for each of the next three days. At the end of each day you will chart the frequency of the behavior you picked to increase. For these first three days you *shouldn't try to increase* the behavior, just simply chart the frequency with which it occurs. Another index card will be used to graph the daily frequency of your chosen behavior.

Part 1
Below is an example of how the index card might look after the three days of counting the behavior you picked to increase.

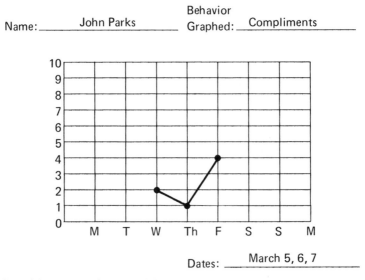

Name: _____John Parks_____ Behavior Graphed: _____Compliments_____

Dates: _____March 5, 6, 7_____

In this example, on Wednesday, March 5, John paid his spouse 2 compliments, on Thursday, the 6th, 1 compliment, and on Friday he paid his spouse 4 compliments.

Part 2

Here you will try to increase the behavior *as much* as you can. Again during each day you will note every time you perform the behavior you chose to increase, and at the end of every day you will chart the total frequency for the day. John's index card might now look like this:

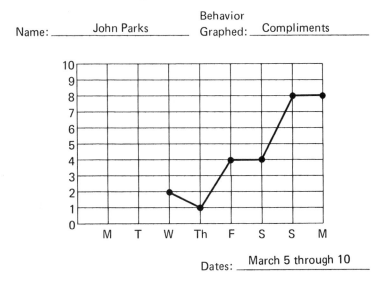

Name: _____John Parks_____ Behavior Graphed: _____Compliments_____

Dates: _____March 5 through 10_____

From the graph we see that John didn't have much success increasing the number of compliments he paid to his wife on Saturday, but doubled the frequency of the three-day counting period on Sunday and maintained this level on Monday.

At the end of the third day of trying to increase your specific positive behavior, ask your spouse to guess the behavior you were working on. Write the behavior your spouse guessed on the back of the charted index card. Was your spouse correct?

MANAGING COMPLAINTS IN THE FAMILY MEETING

The Negative Nebulous to Specific Negative

When you're hurt, or angry, or sad about a problem in your marriage, you will often find it hard to be specific in your complaint. Most people do one of two things when they feel this way and usually state their feelings as a complaint. They use statements that begin with "You never" or "You always." For example, "You never pay any attention to me," or "You always insult me in front of strangers." Or they describe their spouse's negative actions as if they were characteristics. For example, "You're lazy," or "You're insensitive."

It is going to be very hard for most of us to stop expressing ourselves in this way when we feel hurt or angry. But we can learn to take a gripe expressed in the usual nebulous and negative way and try to make it specific. Then, once we've gotten it to be specific and negative, we can work to suggest specific positive things we can do to deal with our spouse's gripe.

Below are the five most frequent communication gripes for husbands and wives based on a study of 792 couples (Burgess, Lock & Thomes, 1971).

Husband's Gripes	Wife's Gripes
Wife nags me.	Husband selfish and inconsiderate.
Wife not affectionate.	
Wife selfish and inconsiderate.	Husband is untruthful.
Wife complains too much.	Husband complains too much.
Wife interferes with hobbies.	Husband does not show his affection.
	Husband does not talk things over.

You can see that most complaints are stated in general terms. It is your job to take one of the gripes and make it specific. That's the first step.

Gripe: "You never pay any attention to me."
Think of a specific instance in which this might occur and make the gripe specific. Use the space below:

"You never ask me any questions about how I've spent *my* day. You usually just tell me about your day." This is an example of a gripe made specific. Can you see the advantage? You know exactly what the complaint is.

Exercise 2   Turning Complaints into Suggestions

When you and your spouse are in a gripe exchange, you will *have to help each other* make gripes specific, and that is a hard thing to do. So try some more examples. Make up a specific gripe for each nebulous gripe and write it in the right-hand column.

Gripe   **Specific Gripe**
Negative Nebulous   *Specific Negative*
  1. You're never affectionate.

  2. You're selfish.

  3. You're inconsiderate.

  4. You're a slob.

  5. You're narrow minded.

  6. You're lazy.

7. You're not very nice.

Stop! If you're having trouble, see the list of specific negative gripes at the end of Exercise 3 (p. 77).

Negative Nebulous   *Specific Negative*

8. You're a weak person.

9. You're immature.

10. You're irresponsible.

11. You're too jealous.

12. You're insensitive.

13. You never listen to me.

14. You don't respect me.

15. You don't love me.

16. You don't care about me.

Compare the specific negative gripes you have filled in above with those at the end of Exercise 3, below.

Exercise 3   From the Negative to the Positive

Let's assume that you've helped make a gripe of your spouse's or your own specific. Your next job is to go from the negative to the positive. Try it.

Specific Negative Gripe	*Positive Suggestion*
You never ask me how my day was.	I'd like you to ask me how my day was.

Get the idea? Now you try. Make a positive suggestion for each specific negative gripe.

Specific Negative Gripe	*Positive Suggestion*
You still haven't painted the bathroom even though you said you would.	
You rarely pay me a compliment.	
You write checks without figuring out the balance.	

Get the idea? OK. Now try it with the specific gripes below.

Specific Negative Gripes

1. You don't touch me, kiss me, or hug me except when you want sex.
2. When you get up from watching TV to get a beer, you don't ask me whether you can get me something too.

3. You invite people over for dinner without first finding out what my plans are.
4. You often don't wear a shirt to dinner.
5. You make fun of my opinions about music.
6. You still haven't fixed the dining room table the way you said you would.
7. You rarely pay me a compliment.
8. You still haven't returned that expensive watch that broke because you say you can't face the clerk.
9. You fly off the handle if we can't afford to buy something we want right away and have to save for it.
10. You write checks without figuring the balance.
11. At a party you get mad if I'm talking to someone else.
12. You keep saying "that's dumb" if you disagree with one of my ideas.
13. When I'm talking, your attention wanders, and you interrupt me or get up and turn on the TV.
14. You never ask me for my opinion on major decisions.
15. You don't want to take me out anywhere.
16. You always take your mother's side in an argument rather than mine.

In your conversation with your spouse you should try to make your gripes specific and you should try to help your spouse make specific gripes. Remember, in order to make a gripe specific:

1. State specifically what it is your spouse does or does not do that bothers you.
2. State the situation that gives rise to the gripe.
3. Give an example of once when it happened. (If this is not possible, say "I'll point it out the next time it happens, OK?")

Remember, to help your spouse make a gripe specific:

1. Ask "What specifically do I do or do not do that bothers you?"
2. Find out in what situations this occurs.

3. Ask "Can you give me an example of once when it happened?" (If not ask, "Well, next time it happens, point it out, OK?")

Exercise 4   Positive Suggestions

Take some time now and practice turning the following specific negative gripes into positive suggestions.

Spouse's Specific Negative Gripes	*Your Positive Suggestions*
1. You rarely pay me a compliment.	I will pay you at least one compliment a day.
2. You write checks without figuring out the balance.	
3. You don't touch me, kiss me, or hug me except when you want sex.	
4. You invite people over for dinner without first finding out what my plans are.	
5. At a party, you get mad if I'm talking to someone else.	
6. You don't ask for my opinion on major decisions.	
7. You don't help me prepare any meals.	
8. You broke the table; you said you'd fix it, and you haven't.	
9. At breakfast you bury your head in the newspaper.	
10. You never throw out your beer cans.	
11. When you drive to school, you often park illegally and get a ticket, which we can't afford to pay.	
12. You never bring the rent over to the landlord.	
13. Often, when I try to study, you decide to vacuum and I can't concentrate.	

14. You haven't cleaned the
    playroom in three months.
15. On Friday, you didn't say
    anything about the dinner
    I spent three hours prepar-
    ing.

Exercise 5   Preparing A Contract

The first step of this assignment is to look through the Up
Deck. You will find this deck in Appendix D. You can cut
it up to make a deck of cards. On each card there is a
behavior that other spouses have described as important in
creating an "Up" feeling in their marriage. Go through the
deck and pick out three major Ups you would like your
partner to do more often.

After you have selected the three Ups you each want
your partner to do more often, exchange the three cards
and select one from your partner's three that you will
agree to do more frequently during the next week. You
must select something to increase which is specific and
observable to both of you.

Again, you should try to suspend evaluation of this
task and give it a good try. *Do not* think of this exercise
as: "I won't try what I agreed to do unless my partner
does his part." Instead, try to think of it as: "We will *both*
try to do our part, and in good faith. I am going to do my
part."

Once you have each selected from your partner's three
cards the one behavior you will increase, enter the specific behavior you agree to increase on the negotiation
form at the end of this exercise. You will often have to
make the behavior more specific than it is on the card.
Then you must each decide on a reward you will receive if
you are successful at increasing each of the Ups. Try
to select a reward for yourself for this first contract that
does not place a burden on your spouse. Some possibilities
which have been used in the past are: an hour or two of
free time on the weekend or evenings to spend alone; buying something new; having your spouse fix something for

you (provided this is not a burden for your spouse!). After you have decided on the rewards you will each receive for fulfilling the contract, enter them on the negotiation form.

Start tomorrow to increase the Ups you have agreed to work on. Place the negotiation form on the refrigerator for the week, or in some other prominent place.

At the end of the week, collect your rewards if you have increased the frequency of the Ups.

If you think your partner is not keeping his or her end of the contract, don't quit doing your end. Instead, schedule a leveling session to discuss the issue.

NEGOTIATION FORM FOR CONTRACTING

Name: _____

Date: _____

Husband	*Wife*
The one behavior I have chosen to accelerate from wife's three cards is:	The one behavior I have chosen to accelerate from husband's three cards is:
_____	_____
_____	_____
_____	_____
The reward I will receive for carrying out this contract is:	The reward I will receive for carrying out this contract is:
_____	_____
_____	_____
_____	_____

Signed _____   Signed _____

5 HIDDEN AGENDAS

WHAT IS A HIDDEN AGENDA?

In most discussions, each person has some issue or agenda that is important. If each person's issue does not get discussed or resolved, it remains hidden. This is called a **hidden agenda.** Conversations with a hidden agenda keep cycling back again and again over the same issue without reaching any successful resolution.

It seems as though you talk about the problem over and over again, yet you don't seem to be getting anywhere, except perhaps thoroughly frustrated. If hidden agendas are allowed to go on undisclosed for several days, weeks, or even years, they will continue to crop up in problem-solving discussions, and they will steer you away from effective problem-solving solutions. Below is a lengthy discussion between a husband and wife. There are also notes to explain how a hidden agenda operates. You will notice that an agenda can be expressed and still remain hidden if it is not discussed.

H: What do you *feel* about the house?

W: What do you *mean,* what do I feel?

H: What do you feel? These possessions; a lot of these possessions are important to you.

W: Not a lot of them.

H: Some of them.

W: Very few.

H: A few of them then.

W: Having a home is important to me, but our issue is housekeeping.

H: Hmmm.

W: I really do know that you're doing more than you should of the housework, and I did read that article.

H: Which one?

W: On a couple that worked out a sharing basis for housekeeping; they split the chores down the middle.

H: That seems fair. Fifty-fifty.

W: Yeah.

It seems at this point that they may be close to a solution.

H: I'd still like to know more of your feelings, though. You know, I don't know . . . I do the work and you act like it's your responsibility.

He's dissatisfied. He still has some issue or agenda that is unresolved.

W: (sighs) What are we talking about right now?

H: Your feelings of responsibility, demarcating what you're responsible for and what you aren't responsible for. You act as if somehow you are in charge, even when I'm doing things.

W: This is a side track, Ted.

H: No it is not. Because when I was cooking the liver . . .

W: That has nothing to do . . .

H: It does. I was cooking the liver and you acted like it was still your responsibility, telling me how to cook it.

He wants to have the authority to do tasks *his* way, without any interference from his wife.

W: Ted, this is a different issue.

H: It is not because you see my goal is to drop the house as soon as possible.

W: But that will never happen in this marriage.

H: Ha ha ha ha ha. You want to go over that again?

W: Yeah. Because, Ted, I am equal to you.

H: Good for you. (sarcastic)

This is her issue. She feels that she is not being treated by Ted as an equal. Now let's see if they give each other's issue a fair hearing.

84

W: And while I agree and know and feel bad about the fact that you are doing *much* more than your share, I don't want to live in a messy house.

H: Honey, I'm speaking from experience. I've had you nag at me about how to do something. That is the real issue.

W: It can't be "my house" that you'll help with.

H: What's distasteful to you is the bad parts of the house. The good parts you like. Do you feel bad about not doing it?

W: Yes I do.

H: Then why don't you do it?

W: I can't. You don't understand that, do you? You never have understood that. You never will.

H: No I don't. I have no intention of spending my life puttering around the house.

Another issue of his is that he would like to see an end in sight to his doing the housework. She, on the other hand, wants him to recognize how serious she is in *wanting* to help.

W: If you have no intention of doing half of the work, who is going to do it? Who do you expect to do it?

H: (coughs) Beats me.

W: Want to try again?

H: Yeah. A maid.

W: A maid?

H: Yes, then I can quit it all. You and the maid can do it then. You can work it out with the maid.

W: And what happens if you can't afford a maid, Ted?

H: Then I'll do half of it. It's as simple as that; but as soon as I can, I'm gonna not do it.

W: Then you have a goal in mind, don't you?

H: That's exactly right; I have a *goal* in mind. I'm only going to pay for 50% of a maid. You can, you can do whatever you want with your 50%, I don't care. I'll help you. You're working, you've got a career. I'll help in part.

W: That's not what I want, Ted; I don't want you to help me in "my chores," because I'm telling you that the role of woman is . . .

H: I don't give a damn about your role.

W: . . . is going to have to stop right here.

H: I don't care.

W: Are you going to accept that?

H: Accept what? Accept what? I don't care about you and your role. You figure that out. You take care of it. Listen, I told you I'd do half until I could figure out a way not to do half, without loading it on you. It seems to me that I'm taking care of your role right there; I'm paying attention to your role.

W: Do you see it as something of us?

H: What? No I don't see it as something of *us*. I see it as something of the house.

His agenda of doing things *his* way has to do with wanting to be an individual with separate authority. He sees her plea for unity as a threat to this. She, on the other hand, sees the plea for unity as a demand for equality and respect.

W: You see, Ted, when we got married, I didn't feel that I became a lesser person.

H: I don't think you became a lesser person either. To me it has nothing to do with *role.*

W: OK. OK. We both hate housework.

H: Yeah.

W: And we're both working right?

H: Yeah, yeah.

W: Why should you say that you're gonna help *me* in the housework?

H: Because . . .

W: Why don't we work together on the housework?

The issue for him is no longer housework.

H: . . . it's your house and not mine.

W: It's my house?

H: As far as I'm concerned it is. *You* were the one who wanted pots and pans, you were the one who wanted . . .

W: And if I hadn't wanted pots and pans, Ted, how would you eat?

H: I don't know. I don't care.

W: When you're cleaning, who are you helping?

H: I'm helping you.

W: You're helping *us.*

H: Us!

W: We're two people living together.

H: Yeah.

86

W: We're an us.

H: Mmmm.

W: We're not one person becoming stronger than the other one, we're two people—*Us.*

H: (disgusted) Us.

W: Coming together as equal people, giving to the other person part of what we are, taking from that person a part of what they are.

To him it seems as if being an "us" means that he will be swallowed up with no individuality or independence. To her it means being loved and respected.

H: Mmmmm.

W: But always to be equal. Different in some ways, but equal.

H: Well, I'll pay for a maid just as any husband pays for a maid, you know.

W: And if you can't afford a maid, Ted, you will work.

H: Well, I'll do my part every day if you do your part.

W: I'll try.

At this point it seems as if the discussion may stop, but it will not because the hidden agendas have not been dealt with.

H: We still haven't solved anything, you know.

W: Why haven't we?

H: You want to have your career and be an equal, and yet you want all the joys and none of the work being "the little woman."

W: What makes you say that? What examples can you give?

H: Concerning the possessions in the house. I mean you're the one who reads *Ladies Home Journal* and *Family Circle* and all that stuff, not me.

W: In addition to other things. They're not my total reading.

H: They're not even *in* my reading.

W: What does that mean, Ted?

H: I don't *know* what it means.

W: Does it mean that because I have an interest in having a home that looks pretty, because I happen to love a piece of wood, a piece of furniture, that I am somehow, what? Men love furniture.

H: Good for them.

W: Maybe you don't, but men love furniture.

H: Good for them.

W: Men love things in the house.

H: I'm glad they do.

W: Why should that somehow be some sign of weakness in me because I do?

H: I don't say it's weakness. I say if you're concerned about it, do something about it. But don't expect me to get all excited.

W: I don't.

H: OK.

W: I don't expect you to love an old chest like I do.

H: OK.

W: And I don't ever ask that from you.

H: Well, I'm willing, if you're working, to help out in the house. And you don't like that phrase.

W: As a part of *our* responsibility.

H: Yeah.

W: To help out in *our* house.

H: I will help.

W: But you'll be helping us, not me.

H: Well, that's what you say.

W: Just like I will help. I will help in the house, Ted.

H: Your part is your part to do. You can use whatever words you want to describe it. I'm using the words that I'm gonna use.

W: OK. We'll make it like fun.

H: But don't tell me how to do what it is that I do.

There's his hidden agenda again.

W: It will be like fun.

H: You can't manufacture something like that. If it's fun, it's fun; if not, it's not.

W: And you can't ever laugh.

H: I can laugh about so much and that's all. Shitty diaper after shitty diaper and it's no fun. (pause) Does it feel to you like we've accomplished anything?

W: What?

H: Does it feel to you like we've accomplished anything?

W: Yeah. The last time we had this argument you got very upset about the fact that I wanted to be treated as an equal human being.

H: Oh ho, that's unfair. All we've accomplished—a word game.

W: *That* was unfair.

This couple was on the way toward developing a perfectly good contracting solution to the housework problem, but their hidden agendas did not get dealt with. So they seemed to go around and around, being unable to accomplish more than what seems like just a word game.

Why Do Hidden Agendas Matter?

We have found that couples who learn the skills in the preceding chapters are often able to have marriages that are smooth and deal well with conflict. However, many of these couples still do not feel very close to one another. They often feel lonely when together, unloved or unloving, cut off from their spouse, or put down. The hidden agenda chapter partly relates to this feeling of closeness, and couples who can recognize and deal with their hidden agendas report feeling "in love" again and the return of romance in their relationship.

A second reason for the hidden agenda chapter is that many couples we have worked with do well using the communication skills of the preceding chapters on most issues. However, there are still some issues (which they usually avoid discussing) on which they fall apart and do not use these skills. We have found that these discussions can be dealt with if the couple is sensitive to hidden agendas. One catastrophic expectation deserves discussion under this second reason. Couples who learn how to deal with hidden agendas and then talk about the scariest issues in their relationship often report that they were afraid that some of their feelings on these issues would destroy everything. After talking about the issues with a knowledge of hidden agendas, they feel a tremendous sense of relief in just getting these strong feelings out into the open. In this way the hidden agenda chapter is related to the leveling chapter.

WHAT KINDS OF HIDDEN AGENDAS ARE THERE?

Let's review a bit. Do you feel that no matter what kind of an agreement you come up with it seems to be doomed to failure? Or do you just go round and round in a conversation, never being able to agree? This may be caused by what has been called a "hidden agenda." The hidden agenda means that while it seems one issue is being discussed, there is actually another issue at stake, one implicit or hidden.

For example, you may be discussing how much time to spend at your in-laws over Christmas. It may be that the issue really at stake for your spouse is whether you care about him or her. Almost anything you say communicates something to your spouse on the hidden agenda dimensions of caring, power, and responsiveness.

Hidden Agendas As Filters

If a spouse has a hidden agenda, he may see all messages through the filter of that agenda. This will set a course of detective work in which the spouse gathers "evidence" about the hidden agenda. The detective work may actually distort the intent of messages and create more Intent/Impact discrepancies. For example, the wife may begin to feel her husband doesn't care about her anymore when they decide to take a skiing vacation mixed with visiting his parents instead of going to the ocean as she suggested. From then on, she begins to gather more instances that she feels confirms the fact of her husband's lack of affection for her. These may now be little things like coming home and kissing the kids before her, or reading a book in the den instead of watching TV with her. The husband may not have intended to give his wife this impression. He would say that he loves her very much. But the important thing is that she feels unloved, and this issue is at the root of every conflict.

Let's pretend to be able to listen in on the hidden agenda and the impact of the following messages.

Message	*Probable Hidden Agenda*
H: I wish you would see a doctor. You look positively frazzled.	W: He thinks I'm unattractive.
W: I don't think we should have another child until I finish school.	H: She doesn't want to stay with me. She's not committed to me.
H: I'm not going to do the dishes.	W: What he needs is more important than what I need.

90

W: I'm tired tonight. I'd rather not have sex.

H: She doesn't care about me.

H: Oh, I'm sorry. I guess I wasn't listening. I've got a lot on my mind.

W: He's not interested in me.

In the first case the wife has the hidden agenda "He doesn't care about me." She may be right. But she may also be distorting messages. Perhaps her husband really was concerned about her health, but she saw it as evidence that he finds her unattractive. The point here is not how he meant the message, or whether or not she is distorting; the point is that the agenda (her issue in this case) has remained hidden. As long as it is hidden it cannot be dealt with. Strong feeling will be associated with the agenda, and every message will seem to have a "message within the message." This may in fact be the case if there is a *shared* hidden agenda. The solution is simply to make the hidden agenda an open real agenda.

These illustrations are not meant to imply what is "really behind" a message, but simply that messages often have impacts on hidden agenda dimensions.

There are three major kinds of hidden agendas we have seen. The most common type is a *positiveness* hidden agenda. Here the issue is *caring*. The filter operating is "My spouse doesn't care about me," and evidence is gathered to nurse this hurt feeling. Every message is weighed or evaluated in terms of this caring filter. The second most common type is a *responsiveness* hidden agenda. Here the issue is *interest*. The filter operating is "My spouse isn't interested in me and doesn't respond to me." Messages are filtered to show this lack of interest or failure to respond. The third type of hidden agenda is a *status* hidden agenda. Here the issue is *power* or *influence*. The filter operating is "I'm not being treated as an equal. I'm being dominated, pushed around." Messages are filtered to show that the spouse is a bully, and messages often seem to convey the hidden message "You are dumb," or "You are incompetent." If you have a hidden agenda, you really feel these things. We don't mean to suggest that you are necessarily distorting messages. We want you to be able to recognize that a message about, let's say, taking out the garbage can have a loaded hidden agenda part to it for you. Learning to recognize these hidden agendas is your task in this chapter.

All hidden agendas can be classified on three dimensions. These dimensions are summarized below and will be expanded.

TYPICAL HIDDEN AGENDA DIMENSIONS

Positive	**Negative**
Positiveness Approach	*Avoidance*
I care about you	I don't care about you
I trust you	I don't trust you
I love you	I don't love you
I want to be with you	I don't want to stay with you
I want to stay with you	I don't like you. You are not
You are attractive to me	attractive to me

Responsiveness

Active	*Passive*
I am interested in you	I am not interested in you
I respond to you	I don't respond to you at all

Status

Influential	*Powerless*
I have influence and status in this relationship	I have less status than you do
What I need is as important as what you need	Your needs come first

Recognizing When You Have a Hidden Agenda

To recognize whether *you* have a hidden agenda, you can ask yourself these questions:

1. Do you feel lonely when talking to your spouse about some things?
2. Do you feel like being alone or with someone else?
3. Do you feel put down, stupid, incompetent, not consulted, not listened to?

4. Do you feel that your spouse is not interested in you or responsive to you?

If so, then you should consider calling a Stop Action and exploring how you feel. *Both* of you may have a hidden agenda if:

1. You have some issues you are just afraid to discuss, issues that are frightening, big issues that you've both been avoiding.
2. You have strong feelings about something that you've been hiding (even out of kindness).
3. You have some issues that you keep talking about again and again, going around in circles, never really making much progress, and both feeling unlistened to and frustrated.

Recognizing a positiveness hidden agenda. Many of the things you say and do have another message in them. When you tell someone something, or simply do something in someone else's presence, you are also communicating:

1. I care about	or	I don't care about you.
2. I trust you	or	I don't trust you.
3. I love you	or	I don't love you.
4. I would choose to be with you	or	I would choose to avoid you.
5. I want to stay with you	or	I want to leave.
6. You are attractive to me	or	You are unattractive to me.

Often when you are going around in circles, unable to reach any decisions or understanding about an issue, there will be a hidden agenda on the positiveness dimensions.

W: Listen, I think we should spend more time together talking.

H: We spend enough time together.

W: We're in the same room, but you're always watching TV.

H: Well I like TV.

W: But I can't talk to you when you're watching TV.

H: You always pick the worst time to interrupt.

W: OK, let's spend some time together not at home. Let's go out.

H: I don't like to go out after a day's work. I'm not the going out type.

W: Well, maybe we could put aside some time to talk together each day.

H: It's so phony to do it that way. Besides, I'm not interested in hearing gossip about Mary's boyfriend.

The message being transmitted here by the husband is one of wanting to avoid talking to his wife. She is thinking "He doesn't care about me."

A positiveness hidden agenda can arise in many situations. However, we have found that it is critical when partners want to exert their uniqueness, and therefore are out of phase. One person wants to be close; the other wants to be alone for some reason. A positiveness agenda builds up.

H: Well, what do you say we make a night of it? Start a fire in the fireplace and have a few drinks.

W: That sounds good, but I'm tired tonight, and I want to finish this novel I'm reading.

H: Finish it tomorrow. Come on.

W: No, I'd really rather not. I'm just not in the mood. (Why doesn't he care about my feelings? . . . he's so bossy) (A status issue)

H: OK, I guess I'll go down to Mike's for a beer. (Oh, boy, rejected again)

Here is another example:

H: At this party let's try to mingle.

W: (He doesn't want to be with me) I'd rather not go if you're just going to talk to other women.

H: (She doesn't trust me) But you ought to learn to meet people.

W: (So you can meet other people) But I'm too shy.

H: (She doesn't trust me at all) Just stand on your own two feet. I know you can do it.

W: (He doesn't like me the way I am) OK, I'll go to the party.

H: Good.

Again a positiveness hidden agenda has been created by the wife wanting to be close and the husband wanting to be independent. He wants to be on his own and she wants to be taken care of in this situation.

Recognizing a responsiveness hidden agenda. Being responsive to your spouse is very different from being positive or saying nice things. It is much harder work. The responsiveness hidden agenda is related to the feeling that your spouse is not really interested in you, not actively engaged with you, that your partner is not responding to you. A responsiveness hidden agenda might go like this:

W: You never talk to me.
H: What's on your mind?
W: It's not what's on *my* mind; it's that I never know what's on *your* mind.
H: What do you want to know?
W: Everything!
H: That's crazy!
W: Here we go again. . . .

This game of hide-and-seek may also go like this:

H: You talk too much!
W: About what?
H: About everything.
W: One of us has to talk!
H: You talk but you never say anything.
W: That's crazy.
H: You're damned right!
W: What do you mean?
H: You make a lot of noise, but that makes it impossible for us to have a real talk.
W: Here we go again.

Remember that a hidden agenda may be operating when you are unable to reach understanding on an issue.

Recognizing a status hidden agenda. In the script below, see if you can spot the point where the conversation first drifts off track.

H: The issue is the house. Right? That it is just a damn mess and I'm sick of it. Something has got to be done. Let me tell you that.

W: OK, as long as it's as equals. We do it as equals, fifty-fifty or not at all.

H: "Not at all" *is* the way it's been, buddy. I'm embarrassed every time my mother comes up here. How do you think I feel explaining to her that we are getting along, that it's OK.

W: Why don't you just tell her the truth?

H: You'd like that, huh? Well, I'll walk out of here before I do. I'm entitled to some privacy you know.

W: Don't threaten me with leaving. Please.

H: That's right. You're the leaver in this family. Are you planning another midnight bus trip?

The husband seems to have stored up a lot of gripes and, although he starts off with the issue of the house being in shape, he soon brings in his embarrassment and his mother. Let's continue with the conversation.

W: The issue was the house. Let's take one thing at a time.

H: Well it's all connected. The house. Clean it up. That's all. Why does it have to be such a big deal? Just *do* it.

W: As long as we share in it equally it's not a big deal.

H: Look, the house is your thing. These possessions mean something to you. But not to me.

W: Not the possessions.

H: You don't care about this place?

W: Having a home is important to me, yes.

H: So there. Now you take care of it. Not fifty-fifty, maybe sixty-forty, but not fifty-fifty.

W: Don't you care about a home?

H: No I don't. Not like you do.

W: But, Ted, I *am* your equal you know.

H: Well good for you. You've come a long way baby.

W: Stop making fun of me.

Can you see the Standoff operating here?

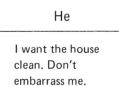

He	She
I want the house clean. Don't embarrass me.	Recognize that I am your equal.

Interest in this Standoff is that neither of them will give an inch until the other sees the impeccable logic of his or her side. What is the hidden agenda for both of them?

H: If she cared about me, she wouldn't embarrass me by having the house so messy. She'd see what pain it causes me. She cares only about herself. (*Status hidden agenda:* Her needs come first)

W: He thinks I am less powerful than he is, that his word should be law around here. Well, I just want equal power and respect. (*Status hidden agenda:* I have less status than he does)

Suppose they were to call a Stop Action at this point. What would happen?

W: OK. Stop Action!

H: Oh no, not again. Cut that junk.

W: Look, we're both in a Standoff. We are.

H: Yeah, we are. OK, let's try that Validation. My side first, OK?

W: OK. You are saying that the house must be neat because it's my thing.

H: No. Well, I did say that, but the main thing is just keeping it clean, see. It's not worth the pain it causes me. See?

W: I see. It hurts you when your snoopy mother comes up here.

H: She's not snoopy.

W: OK, sorry, just concerned then. But it embarrasses you when she asks about us, right?

H: Right.

W: I can see that. OK, let's put an end to that. We'll get the house clean somehow even if we have to borrow money for a maid.

H: Well, we can't do that. But, yeah, that's my side of it.

W: Now, what's mine?

H: That you want to be a liberated woman.

W: Not that pat a thing. Just that I feel put down by your saying the house is all my thing and that I should do it. Having a home is something you do together. See?

H: Yes. You're saying that my putting it all on you makes you feel kind of like a slave, my slave. Right?

W: Well, yeah.

H: Partly I'm just mad at you for other things and trying to get even.

W: Yeah I know.

H: But let's stick to these two issues. Our agenda is getting and keeping the house clean for me, and being equals in having a home together for you.

W: Right.

They are now ready to continue with a Family Meeting.

Dealing with Hidden Agendas

Cutting through "the mustard." "Mustard" is a term we use for what couples sometimes spread over their messages. The mustard makes it hard to know what they really feel. Often they too are unaware of what they feel. It is difficult to teach a person to cut through her own mustard and say what she really feels. But when you do cut through the mustard, the message becomes simpler, clearer, and more direct. Below are some examples to explain this concept. In the messages without mustard we don't mean to say that these are *always* what's behind the message, just what was behind the message in these specific cases.

Message with Mustard	*Message without Mustard*
I'd like to spend as much time with my mother as with yours this Christmas.	When we go to your mother's house you always hurt my feelings, and the two of you gang up on me.
I've tried to be a good husband, and I want you to tell me what I can do to be better.	I am furious at you for not meeting me halfway or acknowledging all I've done.
I'd like to know how you feel.	I'm too scared to tell you how I feel.

Hidden agendas crop up even in the most peaceful marriages but they should never be ignored. They may just signal minor annoyances, but it is more likely that they are flashing red signals indicating that the partner who is doing the clue-dropping is carrying a dangerously ballooning sack of grievances. At any rate, these hidden agenda clues should be investigated for what's behind them. As soon as partners stop putting up with silence, indifference, and camouflaging and learn to fight for clearer communication, tensions seem to clear up. This represents no "cure." When communication channels become unclogged, couples normally find that they are considerably further apart in their ideas for a livable marriage than they want to be; but at least they are no longer kidding each other about their communication gap. Once you are in the position of having cleared up the hidden agendas behind an unresolved issue, the next step is to go on to negotiating an agreement that satisfies both partners.

To deal with a hidden agenda, try to catch each other in the use of hidden agendas and aggressively eliminate their use. This skill will take some practice on your part as both a speaker and a listener. It is easy to fall into the trap of believing you are uncovering a hidden agenda while in fact you are in an *arguing mode.* In the *arguing mode,* you are angry at your partner, and you are not stating your true feelings. Earlier in this chapter we presented a conversation that went as follows:

W: Ted, this is a different issue.
H: It is not because my goal is to drop the house as soon as possible.
W: But that will never happen in this marriage.
H: Ha ha ha ha ha. You want to go over that again?
W: Yeah. Because, Ted, I am equal to you.
H: Good for you. (sarcastic)

It may seem that when this wife said "Ted, I am equal to you," she was in fact trying to deal with a status hidden agenda. However, the wife's statement was in the arguing mode, and the husband responds to the message with his own anger which gets expressed sarcastically. To deal effectively with a hidden agenda, you must state how *you* are feeling. In the above example, one way for the wife to deal with the hidden agenda is to say "Ted, I am feeling put-down, that my needs in the relationship are not as important as yours." With this statement the wife moves out of the arguing mode; she states how the issue is making *her* feel.

When working through hidden agendas, we have also found it useful to call a "Stop Action." Remember that a hidden agenda may be operating when you are unable to reach understanding on an issue. Whenever you have the "here-we-go-again" feeling, say "Stop Action." It is time to change the nature of your communication. At this point ask yourself (and your spouse) how you are feeling. Use the Feeling Chart on page 32. However, it should not limit your feelings. If the way you feel isn't described in the list, add whatever words *do* describe your feelings.

State how you are feeling and ask your spouse how he or she is feeling. You should try to speak one at a time, and for this purpose you can use a checker or bottle cap to indicate whose turn it is to talk. Then, when you decide *how* you are feeling, try to see which feeling will go with which hidden agenda. Try to decide what is making you feel that way.

If you are having trouble deciding on how you're feeling, become more aware of your feelings instead of shoving them underground. It might help to scan your body. Are your muscles tense? How are you sitting? What do you feel like doing right now? What comes to your mind?

Decide on a *change* in *your own* behavior before going back to your discussion after a Stop Action has been called. There are three ways you can change your behavior to have an impact on the flow of communication and to help break up hidden agendas.

1. You have to listen well enough *to summarize* what your spouse is saying. Here is a review of how to build listening skills that may also be helpful:

   a. Speaker speaks.
   b. Speaker checks Impact by asking listener to paraphrase his message.
   c. Speaker corrects paraphrase by stating discrepancies between Intent and Impact.
   Paraphrasing and Check-out should focus on both components of the message: content and effect.
   e. Speaker and listener switch roles.
   f. Process continues.

100

Listening well means that you're not getting ready to disagree with what your spouse is saying, or to show why it is wrong. Below is an example of a couple listening well:

H: I thought when you said that Jimmy should mind his father that you were just butting in on my conversation with Jimmy and telling him I wasn't handling it well.

W: (*Thinks:* That's not the way it was at all. I was just trying to *help* him with Jimmy, who was being a brat.) *Says:* OK, you saw what I was doing as interfering.

H: Right, that's it.

Notice that although she disagrees with his viewpoint she still communicates that his feelings are real and valid. If she had said "No, that's wrong. I was trying to help. Why do you *distort* everything?" he would then probably have said that he didn't distort anything, but that *she* was the one distorting. She would have been telling him that he had no right to have those feelings, and that he was stupid to have them. This brings us to the second point.

2. You have to get out of your own viewpoint and actually try to understand the *validity* of your spouse's viewpoint. Try honestly to see it from your spouse's point of view; communicate somehow that you can see how he or she might feel that way, and that it makes some good sense to feel that way. Accept some responsibility for how your spouse feels. Say something like "I understand how you feel, I see your point of view, and it makes sense to me." This is one form of reinforcing your spouse's point of view or part of it. After you have tried to see the other point of view, or at least found some good in it, *only then* try telling your side of it. Let's look at how these two things, *summarizing* and *validating,* are used in a responsiveness hidden agenda.

W: What do you think the main problem is concerning the way we communicate?

H: Well, when I want to talk to you about something, you usually don't want to.

W: When do I do that?

H: Like the other night; we were in bed, and I thought something was bothering you and I asked, "What's the matter?" and you said nothing. Then I said come on, I know there's something wrong and you said, "I don't want to talk about it."

W: Well, you should know what's wrong!

The couple is stuck. The wife thinks the husband should know what the problem is, and he either won't admit he knows, or has no way of finding out. The hidden agenda underlying the communication problem is not yet clear. Let's have the husband call a Stop Action and see if the hidden agenda becomes clearer.

H: Hey, Stop Action! We're getting nowhere. Let's stop for a minute and think about what the hell is going on.

W: OK, you're right. This always happens and all we do is get upset. I guess the issue is, and you know this, that I don't enjoy sex. I mean, I do sometimes, but most of the time it's not much fun.

H: Well, you're right. I can tell you kind of give in when I want it, but, gee, how do you think I feel.

W: What do you mean? You get what you want—I don't see why you're complaining.

H: Well, I'll tell you why—it's like it's war time and you're rationing sex!

Another Stop Action is called for to unravel the hidden agenda further.

W: Let's call a Stop Action again. We know that this kind of talk will only lead to more fighting.

H: OK, let's find out how we each feel about the issue.

W: OK, I think that my main concern is that you aren't very romantic when we're in bed.

H: You mean that I treat you kind of impersonally.

Note: Here the husband is *summarizing* what the wife said, using different words.

W: Yeah, sometimes I feel kind of used.

H: I can understand that, even though I really wasn't aware of your feelings. I guess I feel that you don't want me around and that makes me feel bad.

W: You're saying that I don't show you that I'd like you to be close to me.

Note: Here the wife is summarizing what the husband said, again using different words.

H: Right. Now we're getting down to the real issues.

The couple is now ready to explain the issues and to reach a solution as the Family Meeting continues.

3. Listening well by summarizing and validating can be done mechanically, or it can be done by actually trying to get out of your own viewpoint. A good way to do that is to ask questions.

H: Well, what were you trying to do?
W: I was trying to help by supporting you against Jimmy. He's been so bratty lately.
H: So you were mad at him, not at the way I was handling it.
W: Right.
H: Then you must have been hurt when I told you not to interrupt.
W: Yes I was. Well, not hurt, but embarrassed in front of the kid, you know, like I was a child, too.
H: Yeah, I can see that. Sorry.

Example of a Common Hidden Agenda: His Wife and His Parents

A hidden agenda we see again and again concerns the wife's in-laws. In this situation we usually find that the wife feels that her in-laws have insulted her, don't like her way of doing things, or don't think that she is good enough for their son. The in-laws are usually feeling bewildered and misunderstood. They feel that their every attempt at reconciliation backfires and is taken wrong. They are sad and feel cut off from their son. The son feels caught in the middle of it all, pulled by two unreasonable parties that he'd like to get together. What usually happens to him is that he tries to be a "translator" who mediates between his wife and his parents. He thinks, "If only they'd listen to each other. Both sides are reasonable. I want them to like each other." On the other hand, his wife and his parents feel abandoned and rejected by him. Everyone is angry at him and he is caught in a trap.

The hidden agenda for the wife is usually: "Whose

family are you in? Are you my husband or their son?" She sees his attempts at being a translator as his supporting them in their attack.

How does this hidden agenda appear on the surface? There may be constant arguments about such issues as how much to visit each set of in-laws at Christmas, or disciplining children, or differences in life style between generations. Beneath it all is the hidden agenda of the husband: "You don't care about me. If you did, you'd try to get along with my parents. You *know* how unhappy it makes me." Her hidden agenda is usually: "You don't care about me. If you did, you would support me when your parents attack me. Whose family are you in, anyway? Do you really accept me? Or are you on your parents' side?"

In our experience, this hidden agenda has never been resolved by the husband's continuing to serve as a translator or mediator between his parents and wife. It can be solved only by directly discussing the hidden agendas. We have seen it solved only when the husband empathizes with and supports his wife. And he must do this publicly to his parents, several times. Then she is on more solid footing with them, and in time the issue can be resolved. This is a painful experience for the husband and he will need his wife's support to get through it. The husband must also support his wife without making her seem like the "bad guy" who is driving him (the innocent) to be mean to his parents. His parents must see that he respects his wife's opinions, and that he expects the same respect from his parents.

After completing these five chapters, we suggest that you go to Appendix B and take the Knowledge Assessment Self-Test to see how well you have learned the material. If you have difficulty with the test, refer to Appendix C, Troubleshooting Guide; it should help you remember the points and it will refer you back to the appropriate material.

6 SOLVING YOUR SEXUAL PROBLEMS

This chapter has one very specific goal: to communicate to you that sexual problems are like other problems in a relationship, that is, they usually have a solution. A sexual problem is not a final end state, like a terminal illness. You may think, "What kinds of people become impotent or have other sexual problems?" The answer is that all kinds of people do. We now know something about how people change unpleasant sexual events into sexual dysfunctions, thanks to the work of people like Masters and Johnson,* Hartman and Fithian, and LoPiccolo and Lobitz. This chapter will draw primarily on the work of these people to give you a sense of what has been accomplished in this area and the methods now available to solve sexual problems. Some of these methods are also useful for enhancing a *good* sexual relationship.

We hope that we can take the mystery out of your notions about sexual counseling. There is nothing magical about a sexual counseling program. However, we want to strongly suggest that you do not attempt to solve your sexual problems on your own, but that you get professional help. We recommend this to you only because *it is so easy to sabotage* a sexual counseling program if you do

---

* Permission for the quotations and figures in this chapter was cordially granted by Dr. William H. Masters and Virginia E. Johnson. The material is from *Human Sexual Inadequacy*, Dr. William H. Masters and Virginia E. Johnson. Boston: Little, Brown and Company, 1971.

not have proper guidance. While this is true of most therapy programs, for some reason it is even truer of therapy with sexual problems. However, we think for this reason, and also *to prevent* the onset of sexual dysfunction, that every couple should be familiar with this chapter.

For example, dyspareunia, or painful intercourse, is one problem that can be either somatic or psychosomatic. A psychosomatic problem does not mean that the pain is not real, or that there is no real tissue damage. It just means that both mind and body are probably involved in the onset and maintenance of the pain. *A medical examination is absolutely essential* in cases of dyspareunia, and recommended for all sexual problems as a sensible beginning procedure. It is important to realize that definitions of sexual dysfunction are not absolute but are related to a particular couple's functioning (see the list of definitions on page 108). For example, a premature ejaculator is defined as a man who ejaculates too soon for his female partner to have orgasm at least 50 percent of the time. Therefore, a man is defined as a premature ejaculator specific to one relationship only. He may not be a premature ejaculator in another relationship.

CHARACTERISTICS OF
SEXUAL COUNSELING PROGRAMS
There are three procedures that sexual counseling programs generally follow when dealing with the various problems they have treated. They are detailed below.

Increasing Communication About Sex Between Partners
Masters and Johnson write:

> It should be underscored constantly that what really is happening in their private sessions of physical expression is that a man and a woman committed to each other are learning to communicate their physical pleasures and their physical irritations in an area that heretofore in our culture has been denied the dignity of freedom of communication. (p. 204)

In fact, most sexual dysfunctions have composite case histories that show how very crucial this lack of communication has been to the development of the sexual problem. This does not mean that both people haven't tried to be kind to one another. However, these very attempts at kindness have often backfired and have had results opposite to what was intended.

For example, in a composite case history of secondary impotence, Masters and Johnson describe a husband who had a few experiences at being unable to obtain or maintain an erection. He began to think about the problem constantly, for example, when driving to work. He asked men his own age how things were going for them, as if his problem were a permanent condition like a terminal illness (age is the mythical scapegoat of many sexual problems). He began to avoid his wife, making excuses about being too tired, or just not interested in sex; the subject was not discussed or even referred to between them. She, in trying to be kind, avoided any physical contact with him, any caressing or kisses that were too long, or touching that might be considered arousing. In doing that, "She makes each sexual encounter much more of a pressured performance and therefore, much less of a continuation of living sexually, but the thought never occurs to her" (Masters and Johnson, 1971, p. 167). They also point out the erosive nature of this lack of communication (even with good intentions) in their composite case history of secondary impotence where an alcoholic episode is a contributing factor (as it was in 35 out of 213 men with a complaint of secondary impotence). They state:

> All communication ceases. Each individual keeps his own counsel or goes his own way. The mutual sexual stimulation in the continuity of physical exposure, in the simple physical touching, holding, or even verbalizing of affection, is almost totally withdrawn.
>
> The lack of communication that starts in the bedroom rapidly spreads through all facets of marital exchange: children, finances, social orientation, mothers-in-law, whatever. In short, sexual dysfunction in the marital bed, created initially by an acute stage of alcoholic ingestion, supplemented at the

107

DEFINITIONS OF SEXUAL DYSFUNCTIONS AND MASTERS AND JOHNSON'S TREATMENT SUCCESS RATE

Sexual Dysfunction	*Description*	*Masters and Johnson's Treatment's Success Rate*
Male		
Impotence		
Primary impotence	Man who has never been able to achieve or maintain an erection of sufficient quality to perform sexual intercourse. Relatively rare problem.	59.4%
Secondary impotence	Man has succeeded in having intercourse in the past. Masters and Johnson's (MJ) definition is inability to get, or loss of, erection beyond 25 percent of his sexual opportunities.	73.8%
Premature Ejaculation	Definition is difficult, but arbitrarily set by MJ as a couple in which the man cannot bring his female partner to orgasm during intercourse at least 50 percent of his opportunities.	97.8%
Ejaculatory Incompetence	Man who does not ejaculate while his penis is contained in the vagina. Relatively rare problem.	82.4%
Dyspareunia	Painful intercourse.	

Female

Primary Orgasmic Dysfunction	A woman who has never had an orgasm in her life even in masturbation.	83.4%
Situational Orgasmic Dysfunction	A woman who has had at least one orgasm, whether through intercourse, self-manipulation, rectal penetration, or oral-genital stimulation.	77.2%
Vaginismus	Muscles of the perineum and outer third of the vagina contract spastically in response to an attempt (or an imagined attempt) at vaginal penetration.	100% relieved of symptoms, 90% were also orgasmic.
Dyspareunia	Painful intercourse.	

next outing by an "I'll show her" attitude and possibly a little too much to drink can destroy the very foundation of a marriage of 10 to 30 years' duration. As the male panics, the wife only adds to his insecurity by her inappropriate verbalization, intended to support and comfort but interpreted by her emotionally unstable husband as immeasurably destructive in subjective content. (p. 168)

You can see from this account the importance of opening communication about sex as a *preventive* measure. We hope that the communication skills you have learned in these chapters will help you to do just that.

A second component of sexual counseling programs involves helping the person deal with his or her own thoughts and fears.

Fear of Performance and the Spectator Role

The way to understand this concept is to give some examples of how it occurs in specific problems. The impotent male, for example, suffers from being too aware of his own and his partner's responses. Instead of being immersed in sensation and the feelings that accompany the erection of the penis, he is so worried about performing that he *wills* his penis to rise. This guarantees splitting him from sensation, making him a *spectator* observing the action, and it also guarantees that he will not have, or will be unable to maintain, an erection. The male is extremely sensitive to fears of sexual performance. And our culture has placed the responsibility for the outcome of the sexual encounter squarely on him. It has also been tied to competence and masculinity in general, and therefore one episode of erectile failure is often a sign that a man is plunging into the abyss of terminal failure and loss of vital powers. It is these very catastrophic expectations, especially when they are not discussed by the partners, which magnify the problem. The next sexual encounter is set up as a test; usually it is unsuccessful, but even if a male succeeds in obtaining an erection, he has failed because he has begun to condition himself as a spectator.

The spectator role is also involved in premature

ejaculation. A common technique males will use to last longer during intercourse is to tense their rectal muscles, and to think about something else in an attempt to halt the flood of sexual sensations. Again the premature ejaculator is training himself to be a spectator. In fact, the training for this problem involves helping the male to get out of the spectator role and to become more aware of the sensations of ejaculatory inevitability. Masters and Johnson describe a composite case history in which the premature ejaculator, through the spectator role, and thanks to an unfortunate lack of communication between husband and wife, becomes impotent.

Once the man experiences premature ejaculation, he begins to worry about it more and more, causing him to adopt the spectator role in every sexual encounter. His partner also takes on the spectator role and begins judging his performance while simultaneously demanding fulfillment and performance.

> Finally, the turning point. The wife pushes for sexual encounter on an occasion when the husband is emotionally distracted, physically tired, and certainly frustrated with his sexual failures. In a naturally self-protective sequence, he is totally uninterested in sexual encounter. When the husband is approached sexually by his demanding partner, there is little in the way of an erective response. For the first time the man fears that he is dealing with a sexual dysfunction of infinitely more gravity than the performance inadequacy of his premature ejaculatory pattern. Once this man, previously sensitized to fears of sexual performance by his wife's repetitively verbalized rejection of his rapid ejaculatory tendencies, fails at erection, fears of performance multiply almost geometrically, and his effectiveness as a sexually functional male diminishes with parallel rapidity. (p. 163)

The third aspect of sexual counseling programs is the enhancement of sensuality.

Enhancement of Sensuality
Most sex therapists say that it is absolutely essential that

111

the enhancement of sensuality be done under conditions of lessened demand for performance. Thus these programs *forbid* sexual intercourse. This is usually a big relief for both partners, and it also allows them to relax and enjoy the sensations and pleasures their bodies can bring.

Often this stage of treatment involves the woman and man pleasuring themselves alone, the exploration of the sexual self. For many people it is a lesson in their own anatomy. For some it also involves a change in what Masters and Johnson call the Sexual Value System (SVS). This system is built into us by our upbringing, and makes us attach labels (usually "No") and emotional reactions (for example, shame, disgust, or guilt) to sexual experience.

Another part of mutual exploration and pleasuring without demand involves each spouse communicating to his or her partner what feels good and what doesn't. It is a reawakening of the senses together with a focus on sensation, and so the sessions are called **sensate focus.** In the sensate focus session, remember that intercourse is forbidden. A sure way to fail is for the couple, or one partner (or the therapist), to decide "tonight's the night" for intercourse. In a sensate focus session one partner is designated as the "giver" and the other the "getter" of sensation. Roles are then reversed. The giver touches and stimulates his or her partner. The breasts and genitals are initially the forbidden zones of the sensate focus, and then later permitted. All clothes are removed, a private place selected where there will be *no* interruptions. Both partners relax. Lotions or oils are recommended (baby oil is fine) to enhance the pleasure of contact. It is the job of the getter to tell the giver what feels good and what doesn't. Often the "getter" might guide the hand of the giver to teach the partner what feels good, especially when caressing the genitals.

THE HUMAN SEXUAL RESPONSE
As part of this chapter's goal to provide some sex educa-

tion, we would like to discuss what is known about human sexuality. Knowing about sexuality may help you realize that sex is an ordinary function of human bodies. Knowing about sexuality may also make it a little easier to talk about the subject with your spouse.

There are four phases of human sexual response: the excitement phase, the plateau phase, the orgasmic phase, and the resolution phase.

The excitement phase is first. When we stimulate each other sexually, we become excited. For women, this phase causes physical changes. The vagina starts expanding and lengthening involuntarily, caused by muscles tightening up inside her. The vagina also starts giving off a liquid which will serve, in the later phases of sex, to make it easier for the penis to enter into it. This is called a lubricant. For men, the excitement phase produces a hard penis (or erection). Penile erection may be lost and regained several times in a prolonged excitement phase. Outside physical interruptions, such as a loud noise, talking about a subject that is different from what is going on sexually, a change in lighting, or a temperature change may cause the loss of an erection even though the penis is being sexually stimulated. Men are much more easily disturbed during this phase. If an erection goes away, it may be a result of the delicate organ he's working with. We must be aware of this fact since many disappointments can be exaggerated and made catastrophic unnecessarily.

The second phase is the plateau phase. Up to this point in time the clitoris has become enlarged and easy for the man to get at; now the clitoris pulls itself into the clitoral hood (the clitoral hood is the foreskin-like covering of the clitoris) and it becomes hard to get at, although it can still be stimulated. (You may want to study the diagram of the female genitals, p. 114.) It may be painful to touch the clitoris itself since it often becomes extremely sensitive. However, stimulation of the general area is all that is required. The front of the vagina begins to swell a little because a lot of blood is going to this area, and the rest of the vagina enlarges a little more. With men, the penis gets a little larger. Basically it increases in diameter. There is also a color change at the head of the penis in most men. The sex flush in both men and women may become noticeable. Gradually the flush will spread over the entire body. A woman's plateau generally lasts longer than a man's.

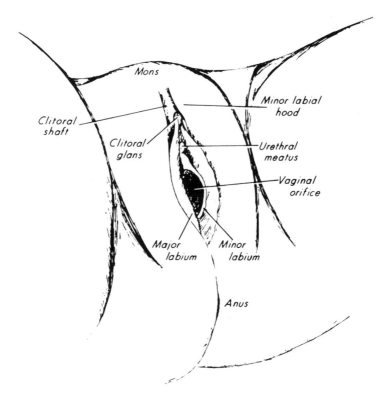

FEMALE PELVIC ANATOMY

The third phase is the orgasmic phase during which the frontal area of the vagina and sometimes the uterus undergoes contractions. These contractions differ from woman to woman, but come at about 0.8 second intervals. They last for different periods of time depending on the intensity of the orgasm. Some women have a feeling of warmth that spreads from the vagina throughout the body. Some women become intensely sensually aware of their whole body. A woman may have one of these sensations or all of them, depending on how she reacts to the orgasm. Women vary a great deal in the kind of experience they have during orgasm. There is really no "typical" or "right" way to experience orgasm since each person is different.

The fourth stage is called the resolution phase. For women, the vagina gets smaller and returns to normal size. In fact, the woman's body returns to the state it was in before the excitement phase. The same is basically true for men.

In all these phases there is a lot of variety between people, making it important for partners to get to know each other's rhythms, what turns them on and off, and so on. There is also a great deal of variation within each person on different occasions. Again, this makes talking about how you feel, or communicating nonverbally, an important aspect of sexual response.

Exploring the Sexual You
An Evening Alone for Women
We are going to suggest a few things you can do by yourself to enjoy your own body, to discover your own joys, beauties, and sensitivities. It is important for you to realize that these suggestions are not a substitute for sexual counseling with professional help. The suggestions we will present are primarily intended to help you reduce your fear about exploring your own sexuality. It is disturbing that when most people are asked to describe their bodies as they see it, they usually have a fairly low opinion of their attractiveness. It is sad that most of us avoid seeing attractive aspects in our own bodies and, in fact, we are usually uncomfortable when we are complimented. We'd like you to put aside your embarrassment about yourself for an evening in which you keep yourself company and introduce your body to yourself. You may feel embarrassed about touching your body for sensual pleasure; many women do. But there really is no logical reason why you

115

shouldn't enjoy yourself.

Take off all your clothes and prepare a bath with your favorite soaps, bath salts, scents, and oils. Wash yourself with your hands, noticing the texture of your muscles and bones. Touch your breasts and notice how they feel. Your nipples may become erect as you rub them. Enjoy these sensations. Pay attention to your genitals. Gently spread the outer lips and wash, focusing on the feelings in your genital and anal area. Take a leisurely bath, then get out of the tub and pat yourself dry.

Get a hand mirror. Sit on a bed or a chair or on cushions on the floor. When you find a comfortable position, use the mirror to look at your genitals. Use the diagram (p. 114). Locate the various areas indicated on the diagram. Start by finding your outer lips (labia majora). Part them and you will see the inner lips (labia minora). Just above the junction where your inner lips meet is the hood of the clitoris (prepuce). Gently pull back the hood and you will see the clitoris. This is the most erotically sensitive area of your body. Explore each area with your fingers, and feel the sensations varying as you touch. Gently slide your finger into the vagina and slowly rotate and slide your finger. Smell your finger when you take it out of your vagina. This is your body's natural odor and there is no need to think of it as something to be covered up.

Continue feeling your genitals and breasts. Use a lubricant if you wish, or saliva; baby oil is a good choice. Caress your thighs and abdomen and vary the speed and pressure of your fingers. Remember, there is nothing to accomplish, no goal. Be kind to yourself and relax. Slide your fingers around the vaginal area and around your genitals to find the motion and rhythm that seems most pleasurable to you. You can try massaging the clitoral area with one hand while stroking the vagina or your breasts with the other; you may try caressing and penetrating your anus. Whatever feels good is good for you.

Continue masturbating until you want to stop. You may or may not experience an orgasm. Remember that

116

orgasms vary. Some are like a form of arousal; some are more vivid and more dramatic. As you approach orgasm your muscles may tense, your breathing may become faster, you may sigh, groan, or whimper. Let yourself go. When you are finished, your body will return to its normal state. If you still feel aroused after a first orgasm, a little stimulation may bring on a second.

Sensate Focus—An Evening Together

You should try this exercise only when you feel comfortable enough to do so. You should both be positive about trying the sensate focus evening, or it may cause a lot of tension. If you do decide to try the sensate focus and you are too tense, just try relaxing your body first. Your therapist can help you with relaxation procedures. We recommend that the therapist use *Progressive Relaxation Training* by Bernstein and Borkovec.

In this exercise you will take first an active, then a passive role. The lights should be on but not bright. Decide first who will be the receiver and who will be the giver. Take off all of your clothes. Practice relaxing your muscles. The first rule is that intercourse is forbidden. The initial sensate focus sessions also prohibit stimulating the genitals and the female's breasts. In later sessions this is permitted. Use a lubricant, such as baby oil, and gently caress your partner's feet, then move slowly up your partner's body. Caress your partner's calves, thighs, abdomen, chest, arms, hands, shoulders, neck, face, hair, back, and buttocks. Take your time and be gentle and creative. Your partner should tell you what feels best. Then receiver and giver should exchange roles. This could be done on another evening.

OUTLINE OF THE TREATMENT OF MAJOR SEXUAL DYSFUNCTIONS

The following material will give you a general idea of how the three major sexual dysfunctions (orgasmic dysfunction, premature ejaculation, and secondary impotence) are treated.

Orgasmic Dysfunction

The first steps for the treatment of orgasmic dysfunction are often similar to the two previous sections of this chapter on "Exploring the sexual you—an evening alone for women," and "Sensate focus—an evening together." The therapists also usually work with the woman's SVS (Sexual Value System) to understand the emotions and thoughts that are developed in the sensate focus exercises. Verbal communication with her partner is encouraged and physical communication is introduced in a nondemanding setting. The next unit of sensate focus is genital manipulation. The nondemand position for this setting entails the husband's sitting with his back against the backboard of the bed. His partner sits between his legs with her back against his chest, her legs draped over his (this position spreads her legs) and with his arms around her. She should lean back and rest her head on his shoulder.

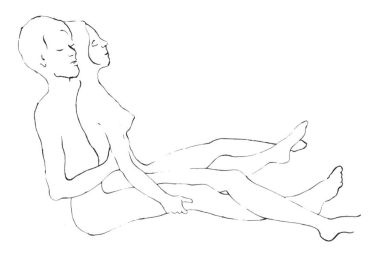

NONDEMAND POSITION FOR FEMALE STIMULATION

She will then lightly guide his hand in an exploration of her genitals. He must not assume any knowledge about what gives her pleasure. It is her job to relax and enjoy the sensations while educating her husband. The usual error that men make is a direct attack on the clitoral glans (unless this is what she wants). Manipulation should be in the general mons area, along either side of the clitoral shaft. The inner thighs and labia are also usually erotic areas. Lubricants are encouraged. An effective technique is a "teasing" approach of "light touch moving at random from the breasts to the abdomen to the thighs to the labia, to the thighs and back to the abdomen and breasts without concentrating specifically on pelvic manipulation early in the stimulative episode" (Masters and Johnson, 1971, p. 303).

After the woman has (following many sessions and roundtable discussions) experienced orgasm, the partners try the female superior position for sexual intercourse.

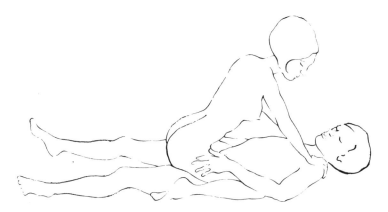

FEMALE-SUPERIOR COITAL POSITION

This is not followed by demanding rapid pelvic thrusting, but by experimental pelvic movements exploring the sensations of containing the penis and coital connection. Women as well as men are discouraged from demanding pelvic thrusting during this phase. Vaginal sensations will increase. Holidays from these sessions are also scheduled in the treatment. Later the couple switches to a lateral coital position.

119

LATERAL COITAL POSITION

Premature Ejaculation

The squeeze technique, developed by James Semans, is a widely accepted therapy for premature ejaculation; it involves a repetitive process based on a system of graduated training and mutual working together, leading to the pleasuring of both partners, and success in controlling ejaculation. But it isn't always easy. Both partners must be willing to devote time and effort. Immediate gratification is postponed for long-term reward and satisfaction. Studies have indicated that anyone can learn to control premature ejaculation.

The set-up. First, the couple finds a place where they won't be disturbed, away from the phone, pets, etc. They relax, perhaps taking a warm, soothing bath together. They also pick a time when they are rested, and they find a place where they will both be comfortable. He lies on his back with his legs apart; she sits between his legs, her feet on each side of his torso. All of these conditions are important. Treatment will not work unless both partners are relaxed and comfortable.

Starting the treatment. The woman begins by pleasuring the man. She takes over while he lies passively, concentrating on his own body. She can start by massaging his chest and stomach, using some pleasant oil or lotion. Then she gently caresses his genitals while he continues to be passive, letting her take over. She continues to pleasure and excite him by stroking and massaging his penis, this leading to an erection. While continuing to have his penis stroked, he finds himself getting more and more aroused. He concentrates on his body sensations, trying to recognize the point of *ejaculatory inevitability,* the point when he can't stop himself from coming, which is usually about fifteen to twenty seconds before he actually does come. It may take him a few times before he can learn to recognize this

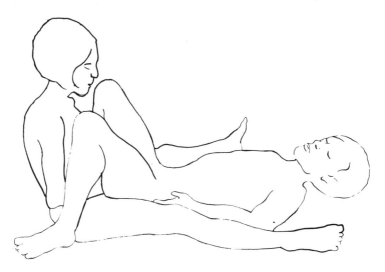

TRAINING POSITION FOR EJACULATORY CONTROL

point, and should he come now, both partners can enjoy his orgasm and try again later. There should never be a sense of disappointment or failure in either partner. It will take time before ejaculation control can be learned. In the meantime, it is important for both people to relax and enjoy each other.

The squeeze. As the pleasuring and arousal continues, and the man gets to the point of inevitable ejaculation, he should signal to his partner—it doesn't matter how—sound, touch, etc. She then proceeds to squeeze his penis by placing her thumb just below the head facing her, with the index and middle finger on the other side of the head; the index finger just above the ridge and the middle finger just below. She then squeezes him gently for 8-15 seconds, or until he has lost 10-30% of his erection. She can modify this technique somewhat by squeezing more firmly for 4-6 seconds, until the erection starts to go down, provided this doesn't hurt. The main thing is to get the erection to go down without hurting her partner. After relaxing for awhile, she repeats the steps of stimulating and squeezing three more times. This constitutes one session.

After three sessions, she goes on to zeroing in. The squeeze technique is repeated, but the penis is squeezed only once, letting it lose its erection. When the penis is soft, but still partially erect, she leans forward and puts the penis into her vagina, remaining still while he gets used to being inside her. After two to three minutes, she starts to gently move; he will get an erection, but he must remain passive. When he reaches the point of inevitable ejaculation, he signals. She gets off his penis and applies the squeeze until he loses erection. She reinserts his penis and begins to move slowly again. After he gets an erection and approaches inevitable ejaculation, the signal is given, she gets off again and again squeezes his penis. This should be done three times per session for three sessions or more.

The female partner must be told before the beginning of the treatment what it will be like for her. It is important that she realize that the object of the therapy is the male partner. Her sexual needs are not taken care of. Often the woman will feel that she is being used. These feelings are not surprising because the man is instructed to concentrate only on his own feelings and sensations. However, it is important for her not to become demanding during the sessions. For example, rapid pelvic thrusting during the latter part of training for ejaculatory control would be detrimental.

Secondary Impotence

An extremely central part of the treatment of impotence involves opening communication between husband and wife, dealing with performance fears, ending the spectator role, and a return to sensations. It is important with impotence, as with other dysfunctions, to realize that "there is no such entity as an uninvolved partner in a marriage contending with any form of sexual inadequacy" (Masters and Johnson, 1971, p. 195). The first step involves convincing the male that he doesn't have to be taught how to develop an erection any more than he has to be taught how to breathe. It is also important to relieve his wife's fears for him about his sexual performance. Sexual techniques include the use of the "teasing" method in a slow, nondemanding fashion consisting of manipulative play to erection, stopping the play to allow a period of distraction in which the male loses the erection, then a return to the play and resurgence of the erection. The male knows intercourse is prohibited, and learns that he can easily achieve more erections.

In later sessions, the wife places herself in the female superior position with her knees below his nipple line before she begins penile manipulation. When a full erection is obtained, she mounts, but uses a "quiet vagina" technique which is nondemanding. While inserting she continues manipulating his penis; later she concentrates on the feeling of containing the penis. The husband can thrust slowly.

Vaginismus and Dyspareunia

Vaginismus can usually be helped by the use of Hegar dilators in graduated sizes. This should be done with assistance from a therapist. The important step in the treatment of vaginismus is an explanation of the psychophysiology of the problem, what it is, how it developed, assurance that relief is possible and, most importantly, a demonstration of the clinical existence of the problem. This usually surprises both partners. Dyspareunia should be dealt with first by a physical examination. Dyspareunia may also involve insufficient vaginal lubrication, a lesbian orientation, a deep-seated lack of identification with her partner, or fears of deep penetration, pregnancy, or sexual inadequacy.

SUMMARY

We hope that this chapter has given you some idea of how the treatment of sexual problems works. Knowing about the therapy won't spoil it for you—it will help take the catastrophe out of the problem. Sex counselors see these problems every day and they have confidence and experience in solving them. So don't panic about sexual problems. Most problems have two things in common: you are not the only one who has ever had the problem, and, most problems have a solution.

7 GETTING THROUGH A CRISIS

This chapter offers suggestions intended to provide structure during times of crisis. We have found that couples in crisis experience a great deal of relief when they decide to follow some guidelines that make sense, reestablish politeness, and begin a process of problem solving. It is important to recognize that these solutions are intended as *temporary* measures to get through a crisis. Once the crisis is past, you can return to working on the communication skills in this book.

DE-ESCALATING QUARRELS
Below are several suggestions that may help *avoid* quarrels or keep them from escalating.

1. If something else is bothering you, if you've had a rough day for example, instead of taking it out on your spouse, say "I've had a rough day and I'm in a bad mood. Don't take my bad mood personally."
2. If you feel yourself getting your dander up, or getting ready to strike out, or to be mean, first ask yourself:

   Is it really worth it to start a fight about this? Is this important enough to argue about?

   If not, hold your tongue. You've edited successfully. If it is, can you say it politely?
3. One basic politeness you may find helpful is suggesting a cooling off period if a quarrel is escalating out of control or not getting anywhere. You can say, "I'd

125

like to stop and cool off. Let's agree to talk some more in an hour." You can make an agreement to postpone your argument to an appointed time for a Family Meeting. In this way, a quarrel will be more likely to become a discussion.

A first step to keep quarrels from escalating is to learn to rewrite the scripts of other couples. Each of you rewrite the following scripts alone and then discuss the rewrites with your spouse.

Instructions: Rewrite the conversations below so that quarrels have less chance of escalating. Change only the statements of the husbands if you are a husband, and only the statements of the wives if you are a wife.

Your notes

H1: (angrily) I just got the bank statement and once again you spent too much. It seems that . . .

W1: (interrupting) I've told you until I'm blue in the face that you should let me know what I can spend.

H2: (getting madder) You got some nerve—you know when you're spending too much! You just don't give a damn!

W2: That's a lot of crap—anyway, you're supposed to handle the money around here.

H3: That's a joke. You wouldn't do anything I tell you anyway.

W3: (sarcastically) Try me!

H4: Oh, hell, it's no use talking to you.

W4: Here we go again.

W1: (angrily) You didn't clean the living room like you said you would!

H1: Uh uh.

W2: Why don't you even say anything to me when I'm upset.

H2: I'm sorry you're upsetting yourself. Really I am.

W3: Don't treat me like a child. I have a right to get sore at you. You never show any interest in the house or in me.

H3: (sweetly) Honey, you're just tired and upset, that's all. Go to sleep. You'll get over it.

W4: Oh God! You don't understand. (turns away)

If you feel that you have mastered this process, then continue reading. If not, turn to the end of the chapter (p. 135) and work on the remaining scripts.

ETIQUETTE FOR THE HOME

A few simple suggestions on etiquette will provide a great deal of relief from quarrels. Below are suggestions that you can modify for your home to fit your own life style, but first try them as they are written before you modify them.

Politeness at the Dinner Table

1. Show good dress and grooming at meals.
2. Find something to like about the meal, and comment on it (food, table arrangements, timing).
3. Conversation should stay clear of difficult issues (household chores, child rearing), and complaints should be avoided. Put-downs are out.

4. Conversation should be pleasant. Some possible topics are current events, undemanding and pleasant information about the day's happenings, TV programs, books, civic problems.
5. Sit facing each other.
6. Relaxed quiet is acceptable; there is no need for conversation all the time.
7. Happy reminiscences are encouraged.
8. Stories about other people are encouraged.
9. Share the chore of clearing the table and doing the dishes.

Politeness When Watching TV

1. Everyone chooses a seat with a clear view.
2. If you are going to get a snack, ask if anyone else would like a similar snack.
3. If someone brings you a snack, express your appreciation.
4. Everyone should clean up the things he (she) has used in the room (dishes, etc.).
5. Conversation should be pleasant and not interfere with another's enjoyment of the TV.

Politeness in Discussion

1. No fits of temper. If you feel a blowup coming, leave the scene and go for a long walk.
2. Only discuss controversial issues when seated at a table facing each other.
3. Do not interrupt the other person. (Say, "Are you finished?" if you wish to speak, and only begin if your spouse says "Yes.")
4. If you are wrong, admit it.
5. Begin in a friendly way.
6. Do one problem at a time. Keep the conversation On Beam.
7. Try honestly to see the problem from the other person's point of view (empathize).
8. Do not put yourself down.
9. Make as many positive suggestions as possible. Accept

128

the other person's suggestions and build upon these suggestions.

See the end of this chapter for an exercise on "keeping track of editing" (p. 141).

HANDLING CRISES

The first step toward handling a crisis is to call Stop Action. Remember that every problem usually has a solution, and often several solutions are likely to work. Even an imperfect solution is better than nothing.

Next, you have to be *active.* Being depressed and hoping things will take care of themselves will not work. Remember, the problem has a solution and it is better to be active and wrong than to be passive and stew about your trouble.

Finally, you have to be agreeable. You may usually be pigheaded and stubborn, and in a crisis you may feel hurt and wronged. However, both of you will have to be agreeable to *some* suggested solution.

Seven Suggestions

The first thing to do in a crisis is to try to bring about some immediate relief for yourself and your spouse. Below are seven suggestions for exiting out of a crisis.

1. *Set ground rules.* Set ground rules of interaction. *No more of Behavior X* is a ground rule in which the most frequently displayed problem behavior of each spouse (which usually serves to escalate the negative exchange) is eliminated. You'll need some way to keep a record of the problem behavior whenever it occurs. Whenever it does occur, you should point it out to one another.

2. *Define structure.* By whatever means, set roles for behavior and interaction both inside and outside of the home. Restrict interaction; ritualize the rules for initiating interaction, terminating interaction, heading off escalating quarrels, protecting "territoriality," and making decisions. Forbid specific kinds of time

together which typically produce high conflict (for example, sexual intercourse can be forbidden).

3. *Stop Action. Stop* certain types of interaction as they occur.

4. *Shaping.* Once you and your spouse begin to act even *slightly nicer,* give out praise and rewards, support and attention. You can strive for a different goal once things have become a little better. Appreciate (and show it) those things that your spouse does that you like.

5. *Stop acting out.* One of the central ideas of the crisis intervention must be to stop "acting out" behaviors. Acting out means doing desperate things in response to feeling desperate. For example, the wife may run away, the husband may try to kill himself, and so on. *These behaviors must stop!* Therefore, one of the central points in the *crisis intervention contract* is:

No acting out,
Just talking out

This must be a basic ground rule.

6. *ABCD analysis.* Once you get through a crisis, it may be good for you to do an ABCD analysis:
Antecedents. What things led up to the crisis? What were the stresses on both of you at the time, both inside and outside the marriage?
Behaviors. How did each of you try to cope with the stresses? How did you each act? What were you thinking?
Consequences. What were the consequences of these actions and thoughts?
Do differently. What could you *do differently* now? What alternatives do you now see?

7. *Negotiate a temporary agreement.* Below is an example of a crisis contract negotiated between a husband and wife that had the objective of politeness. The contract was posted on the refrigerator.

Temporary Contract

WE, the undersigned, in order to form a more harmonious union, do hereby agree and contract to:

1. Neither make nor give any general summaries of the other's behavior, to include:
   a. No accusations
   b. No ascribing of motives
2. Talk neither of separation nor of any future qualitative possibility, i.e., no discussion of future quality of life until the May 15th meeting.
3. In discussion of the problem, stick to the specific situation, making sure by appropriate questions that the other understands exactly what is meant, i.e., that each is discussing the same specific situation.
4. If appropriate, analyze moment by moment how or why any argument, discord, or misunderstanding arose.
5. In regard to (3) and (4) above, validate the discussion of each by each communicating an understanding of the other's point of view, and allowing that understanding to be corrected.
6. Allow each partner a time in the evening:
   a. to be alone
   b. for trivia
   c. to relax
   d. to talk of the day's events
7. Do not press a discussion if the other person resists discussion. If this situation should arise, each will have the right to ask for an appointed time, with negotiable time limits, when problems that either of you thinks are important will be discussed. The party of whom an appointed time is requested must grant it.

Payoff for husband at end of month: new pipe, up to $10.
Payoff for wife at end of month: new records, up to $10.

PERSONAL PROBLEM SOLVING

Some couples experience a crisis situation because they have not developed effective ways of solving personal problems. Whereas the above seven suggestions are especially useful for dealing with the first recognition of a crisis situation, the following guide to problem solving may be useful for changing the conditions that gave rise to the crisis.

The first thing you need to do is to realize that you are helpless but not hopeless. You should try to pretend, even if you don't believe it, that the cause of your problems is that you and your spouse have not yet found the right solution to your problems (you are helpless) rather than that your problems have no solutions (you are hopeless). You should tell yourself "We are helpless because we haven't found the right tool for solving our problems *yet*."

Five Steps for Solving A Personal Problem

Review your outlook. If you approach the problem as a hopeless situation, you have already lost half the battle. Problem situations are a normal part of everyday life, and they occur in all marriages. Though some couples are able to solve their problems easier, all couples can learn to solve their problems effectively. In this first step, pause and try to make your outlook positive. Think about your problem situation instead of acting out hasty solutions, or arguing about who is right or wrong.

What is the problem? The goal of step two is to specify the problem very carefully. The importance of making a specific and complete description of a problem situation cannot be overemphasized. The following questions may help you to identify *the specifics* of the problem confronting you:

1. What are we having difficulty handling (i.e., what is the problem)?
2. In which situations does the difficulty appear? (It is helpful to pick a particular situation in which the

problem occurred. In this way you can focus on an example of the problem and work towards a solution of the problem in each specific instance.)

3. Where does the problem occur?
4. When does the problem occur?
5. Who else is present when the problem occurs?
6. What do I do when the problem occurs?
7. What does my spouse do when the problem occurs?
8. What would I like to change in this specific example?
9. What is preventing us from solving our problem?
10. If you had a magic wand, and could solve the problem magically, what would the outcome of the problem situation look like?

How can we solve the problem? Try to think of as many possible solutions as you can. Some solutions will seem better than others, but at this point try to list as many possible solutions as you can think of. Don't evaluate them until you've listed all solutions that come to mind.

Look over your list and predict what would happen if you tried each solution. Ask yourself "What would happen if we tried that?" "How would my spouse feel if we worked on this solution?" "How would I feel?" Cross out all the solutions that you believe will bring undesirable consequences. When you are left with a list of "good possible solutions," evaluate each of those to select the best alternative. The solution you select should result in the best outcome for you and your spouse; it should also be the most practical.

Working with the best possible solution. The best solution may have several parts, or it may prescribe a series of related actions. Decide between you how you are going to implement this solution. With as much detail as possible, plan the action you are both going to take. Remember, be as specific about what you are going to do as you can. Work together with your spouse to outline which behaviors you each will do to carry out your best possible solution.

Trying out the best possible solution. After you have gone through a specific situation in which you've tried out the solution, discuss with your spouse whether the problem situation changed in the way you both desired. If you were successful, congratulate each other and plan a method for maintaining the solution.

What if the solution did not work? If the solution you tried out did not work, this *does not* mean you can't solve the problem. *Don't give up.* You can try any of the following alternatives if the problem solution didn't work:

1. Go back to page 133 (Working With the Best Possible Solution) and revise your plan of action.
2. Go back to page 133 (How Can We Solve the Problem?) and review other possible solutions. Perhaps you didn't pick the best one before; pick another one now.
3. Look at the definition of the problem, page 132 (What is the Problem?). Were any important facts left out? Perhaps you need to redefine the problem. Recognize that it may take several tries. You may have to "start small" and solve your problem step by step.
4. Use the five steps of problem solving to help you find another solution.

When you try this method for solving a personal problem, it is important to *actually go through* the steps described above. The best way to do that is to schedule a Family Meeting with your spouse when you are sure you will have the time to go through the steps carefully.

Remember, *you need to adopt an experimental attitude.* You will also have to postpone your evaluation of a solution until after you've tried it.

Exercise 1   Escalating Quarrels

(Refer to page 125 on de-escalating quarrels.) Discuss your notes with each other. If you have trouble, go back to the "do's and don'ts" (p. 47) and the suggestions in the editing chapter (Chapter 3).

Dinner Table

H1: You smoke too much.

W1: But I've got those new fil-
ters.

H2: You're just kidding yourself.

W2: You know I just can't stop.
I'm not a strong person.

H3: Yeah, but I don't like your
smoking. It gives you bad
breath.

W3: Well, I don't like your beer
belly. Why don't you stop
drinking beer?

H4: It's your fault because you
feed me fattening things
like this dinner tonight,
which, by the way, was over-
cooked.

W4: Well, get yourself a new
cook, fatty. (she leaves the
table)

Driving Home From a Party

W1: (angrily) I'm never going to
a party with you again. You
paid no attention to me and
everybody saw it. I feel so
worthless . . . (starts crying)

H1: Stop crying! You always
cry when you try to get
your way. No wonder the
kids cry all the time.

W2: It's a helluvalot better to
cry than to drink all the
time like you do. You spend
all our extra money on
whiskey.

H2: You should talk—you spend
more money at the hairdresser than I do on booze.

W3: (crying again) At least my
hairdresser pays attention
to me. That's more than I
can say for you, you louse.

H3: (trying to concentrate on
the road) Listen, all I want
to do is drive home quietly,
but you just talk, yak, yak;
when we have an accident,
it will be your fault.

W4: Oh hell, shut up yourself.
(continues to cry)

(silence)

Breakfast Table

H1: Why in hell don't you ever
put out napkins for breakfast?

W1: Because it's not necessary. I
never spill anything on
myself.

H2: (getting angry) I'm not talking about napkins for you.
I'm talking about napkins
for us.

W2: (sarcastically) I haven't
noticed that you spill anything either.

H3: (angrily) So what! I like to
wipe my mouth after I eat.

W3: (loudly) No sir! That's not
it at all. I know what it is—
you just like to nag me.

H4: You're ridiculous—you want
to be nagged. That's why I
can't get anything until I
yell about it.

W4: Oh, you really like it.

H5: Like what?

W5: (losing temper) You jerk—I mean like yelling at me.

H6: To hell with you! I'll eat breakfast at the office. (leaves)

W6: (yelling after him) You're crazy!

Living Room

Your notes

W1: You never listen to me.

H1: I don't want to talk to you now.

W2: You really don't care what I think; nothing I say is important.

H2: Listen, don't hassle me. I've had a hard day and I'm not up for your bitching.

W3: You're just like your mother. Insensitive and stubborn.

H3: Don't bring her into this. Your family is nothing to brag about; it's their fault you're the way you are.

W4: Don't blame my family, smarty pants. This is your fault for being such a rotten husband.

H4: You think you're a prize? You got a lot to learn, kiddo.

W5: (starts crying and leaves room)

Living Room

Your notes

H1: Bring me a cup of coffee!

W1: Get it yourself, you lazy
bum. I've been on my feet
all day.

H2: Don't ever ask me to do
something for you, you
bitch.

W2: Don't worry, you never do
anything for me anyway.

H3: You can forget about getting that new coat for your
birthday.

W3: Oh, yeah? Well, Mr. Money-
bags, I'll just write out a
check and get it myself.
So there!

H4: You do and I'll break your
neck.

W4: Just try it, buster. Just try
it.

H5: (smashes table lamp in living room)

W5: (runs out of house)

Living Room

Your notes

W1: We need a new refrigerator.

H1: There you go again with
your constant demands.

W2: If you made a little more
money we'd have more.

H2: I make enough. You're just
a spendthrift.

W3: You're scared silly to ever
ask for a little raise.

H3: I'm not scared to walk right
out on you.

W4: Go ahead and leave! You're
no good to me anyway.

H4: Well, I'm taking all this
stuff with me. I bought it.
It's all mine.

138

W5: It's half mine by law.
H5: Here take half of this end
table. (smashes table)
W6: I'm calling the cops! (locks
self in room)

Driving

Your notes

H1: Mary, slow down or you'll
miss that turn.
W1: George, stop telling me how
to drive.
H2: It's just that you're so
absent minded.
W2: I'm a good driver.
H3: Not in my book you're not.
You don't concentrate when
you drive.
W3: I also don't take chances
the way you did yesterday.
Passing in a no passing zone.
H4: There, you see, you missed
that turn. I told you you'd
miss it!
W4: I told you so, I told you so,
you smart ass! I wouldn't of
missed it if you'd quit
pickin' on me.
H5: Next time I'll drive.
W5: You can drive right now.
I'm pulling over.
H6: That's OK with me.
(both silent)

Living Room

Your notes

W1: I would like to watch this
special on raising kids.
H1: Not till the game's over.
W2: I think we should *both*
watch this show.

139

H2: Game'll be over in an hour
or so.

W3: That'll be too late. You've
been watching games *all*
day.

H3: *This* game is the one I care
about.

W4: You don't care about a family at all, do you?

H4: Not as much as football—
now beat it.

W5: Oh, you're so smart, such a
big shot!

H5: Leave that dial alone!

W6: No! Get out of my way!
Where are you going?

H6: I'm gonna watch it at Nick's.

W7: Damn you!

Dining Room

Your notes

H1: Hi, what's for dinner?

W1: Where have *you* been? You
are late.

H2: I got caught in traffic—I'm
not all that late anyway, so
don't get in a huff.

W2: Well, you're just inconsiderate. Just take a look at what
you've done to my roast!

H3: Ugh! It's not done the way
I like it. It's well done, not
medium rare. What happened?

W3: What *happened?* It was
beautiful 45 minutes ago
when you *promised* to be
home. Why didn't you at
least call?

H4: I couldn't. I got caught in
traffic! How many times do
I have to tell you?

140

W4: You could have called.
You're just insensitive to
my feelings!

H5: I could not. Besides, why
did you put the roast in so
early, anyway?

W5: Oh, so now it's my fault! If
you had just one inkling of
consideration in your whole
body, you'd have called me.

H6: Well, if you knew anything
about cooking, you wouldn't
have ruined our dinner!

Exercise 2   Keeping Track of Editing

Take an index card and mark off the days of the week as
in the example below:

EDITING CARD

Editing Points

Mon: ⊬⊬⊬ I
Tues: II
Wed: III
Thur: IIII
Fri: II
Sat: ⊬⊬⊬ ⊬⊬⊬ ⊬⊬⊬
Sun: ⊬⊬⊬ ⊬⊬⊬ ⊬⊬⊬ ⊬⊬⊬ I

Each mark on the card indicates a time that you have
successfully edited.

Before the weekend, list the problem situations that
you can anticipate coming up over the weekend, then
decide what you can do in each situation to avoid trouble,
blowups, or arguments. Over the weekend, keep track of
your editing points by having your index card and a pencil
in front of you during a discussion with your spouse, and
suggest that your spouse do the same.

8 MAKING A GOOD THING BETTER

We should say at the outset that this was the hardest chapter for us to write. We are still searching for answers in the area of increasing intimacy. What we have to offer here, we offer with humility. These are suggestions that have some meaning to us. Pick and choose, and remember to postpone evaluation until after you have tried a suggestion.

WHAT IS THE PROBLEM?

The problem was expressed recently in a Public Broadcasting System television screenplay called "Double Solitaire," based on the 1971 play by Robert Anderson entitled *I Never Sang for My Father,* in which the wife says to her husband that she feels that they are like two train tracks going in the same direction forever, but never really touching. Even if you feel that your marriage is "basically OK," think about the descriptions below to see if you experience any of them altogether too often.

1. You feel lonely.
2. You feel like something vague is missing.
3. You don't know who you are with your spouse.
4. You don't think your spouse really knows who you are, or wants to know.
5. You feel resentful because your spouse isn't really interested in you, in your inner life.
6. You feel trapped by all your roles, as if you're caught somewhere inside these roles

143

7. You feel unfree.
8. You feel dead.
9. You feel withdrawn and cut off from your spouse.
10. You feel that your life together is meaningless routine.
11. You feel that there never seems to be time in your life for leisure or joy, day to day.
12. You feel that your problems may be beyond resolution, or that you are basically incompatible.

These are some of the general indications that intimacy or closeness is an issue between you and your spouse. What can you do? First of all, do you want to do anything about it? That's not an easy question to answer. But let's assume you decide you do want to try (even if you're not *totally* convinced that it's a good idea).

GENERAL STRATEGIES

There are two general things you need to do. First, you have to begin by caring about yourself, by thinking of what *you* need, and about the kind of life *you* want for yourself. You must be selfish, not selfless. This means a commitment to your own personal growth and enhancement, your own creativity. It means finding out who you are and what you need. And that usually means you have to like and respect yourself.

Maybe that first piece of advice sounds peculiar. To achieve intimacy, I need to be selfish? We find that couples who have become closer to each other instead of living in "double solitaire" actually have become more independent of one another. They find themselves good company, but they value other people as well as solitude.

Second, let us suggest that you and your spouse try an exercise separately. Write down what it is that you have had together that was precious. Can you recall those moments when you really talked to one another, or enjoyed an event together? Make a list of such times.

After you do that, share your lists. Have you noticed that you've stopped doing those things together, or doing them in the same way you used to? What are the conditions under which the two of you come together now? Is this a strange question? Perhaps it is because you take your being with each other for granted, as a given, as a matter of course. You are together because you live that way; it is a habit. You do not make time to come together to talk, to share your worries, your dreams, to do things together, to fingerpaint, to take simple joys with each other.

So, second is the nature of your coming together. This is really about responsiveness to one another, about interest in one another, about friendship.

These are the general strategies we offer to you with humility. It's an outline that needs to be filled in with your own creativity. Following are some specific suggestions that may give you some ideas.

INTIMACY
There are things that couples do to increase intimacy that they rarely talk about with other people, things that really involve being good friends. After we list some of these ideas, we will offer suggestions for increasing closeness. Below is a description of the things we've found that spouses do who like each other. They spend time just talking to each other. The talk does not always involve errands or getting things done; basically it involves sharing each other's inner life.

1. Couples will spend time planning about the future, not to solve problems but to consider alternatives. They share goals, dreams, plans. They may discuss a question like "What would you like to be doing five years from now?" This discussion may have the character of a fantasy. It is an exploration of each other's wishes, hopes, and worries.
2. Couples will also spend time reminiscing about the past. At times this may lead to discussions about how to change the present.
3. Couples will talk about each other to understand themselves, as a joint venture. For example, the

husband may talk about his childhood and his wife may be a partner in his attempt at understanding himself better. He may, for example, find that he misses certain of his parents' traditions, and they may decide to try returning to these traditions.

4. Couples also share fantasy. We will elaborate on this idea further on, but basically it involves creating inner experiences together. Children who are best friends do this in their play. Some adults discuss last night's dreams in the morning and try to figure out dreams together. Some couples will also pretend that they are doing something new and exciting. Much like making up a story together, a couple may pretend to take a trip to Norway while actually sitting together in their living room.

5. Couples will often share silliness, speak in special voices, make up special characters, strike characteristic facial expressions which communicate special meanings, and use telegraphic language which evokes memories of previous events that only they share. For example, the husband of one couple we knew would pretend to be Colonel Lee, the rooster, and do a "Colonel Lee act" on special occasions. This act involved special voices and facial expressions, but was always extemporaneous and lots of fun for both him and his wife.

6. Couples will also engage in a shared deviant experience. For example, we know one couple who would go to a shopping mall, find another couple that looked different from them, and follow them around all day doing exactly what they did. Sometimes they pretended they were CIA spies in this activity. But it remained their own shared secret.

The quality of these experiences that close couples have, although infrequent, seems to be very important to them. The next section gives some specific suggestions for increasing intimacy.

146

SPECIFIC SUGGESTIONS

After completing the previous chapters, some couples say "We accomplished changes in our marriage, that's true. And a lot of them didn't seem possible when we started. But things are often still pretty dull."

This section has to do with the exploration of new ideas for your marriage—and with intimacy. We offer our suggestions, and hope you will find some of them useful. We will also refer you to other material rather than summarize or duplicate what others have done well.

First, a word of caution about intimacy. In a good relationship, you will find cycles of closeness and apartness. People need some "breathing room," separateness, and independence. So if you are seeking an intimacy that is intense all the time, you are apt to wind up very disappointed.

How to Have Enjoyable Conversations

Getting started. Some people talk a blue streak while others often have trouble knowing how to get started. This section is for those quiet people who sometimes have it rough because they are so hard on themselves. They think over what they are going to say for so long that they never say it. The longer they are quiet, the harder they are on themselves and the harder it becomes to say something. After a long silence, a quiet person often thinks that what he says must be a jewel, a pearl of wisdom. Noisy people, on the other hand, talk and talk. Most of what they say is junk and has no impact on other people. But that is OK. They have a low hit rate, but they produce enough words so that some of what they say is good.

You cannot assume that your spouse knows what's going on in your mind, what you did today, what you are worried about, or what your plans are. Maybe you sometimes don't know what to talk about, and don't know what to say to make the time pass pleasantly. Below are some suggestions you can use to increase your conversational skills.

Suggestion 1   Speak and Respond

Speak. You will ease tension a lot if you just *talk.* Talk about what you are doing, what you just did, what you are planning to do. Talk about what you are thinking about, what you are feeling, what you are concerned about. *Be specific.* What were you doing, thinking, or feeling just before you and your spouse got together?

A good way to start is *to find the common ground* between you. For example, if you are both hungry and it is before dinner, you can talk about food, or where to go out to eat, or which place in town is best to eat, and which place is the worst.

Don't be afraid to say something you think sounds dumb. People say dumb things all the time and it's OK. It's a starter of conversation, and you are being considerate and easing the other person's tension; *the other person is probably also worried about the same things.*

Respond. If your spouse says something, react to it and you will be able to keep the conversation going. Say something that relates to what your spouse has just said.

Just as you began the conversation by talking about what you were thinking, doing, or feeling before the meeting, you can now react to what was said, how it makes you think, feel, or what it makes you want to do.

Suggestion 2   Active Listening

Being a good listener is important in conversation. Most people are *passive* listeners. They may grunt or say "yeah" and "uh huh," but they have a blank expression on their faces that seems to tell you they are miles away and couldn't care less about what you are saying.

Being an active listener means responding with your head, with your eyes, with your facial expressions. Communicate that you are tuned in. Try to maintain eye contact when listening. Try not to have a blank look on your face.

A second vital part of active listening is asking questions. When someone is talking to you, it is as if they are a

148

tour guide leading you on a tour. Think of yourself as a tourist. A good tourist *asks questions.* First ask yourself, "Do I *really* know what the other person is referring to?" Usually you do, but often a dumb question will help a lot. For example,

> "I ate in one of those old restaurants with the funny waiters."
> "Yeah."

the response may seem empathic, but it stops conversation. Try:

> "What were the waiters like?"
> "Oh, they were dressed up like musicians at a concert, sort of in tuxedos. And very proper and formal, you know . . . ."

This question leads you further along on the tour. Don't assume you know what your spouse means, or that your spouse's experience is just like yours. Your greatest tool in asking questions is your own ignorance. So ask, be dumb; find out what your spouse means.

Meaningful conversation. Many of the principles for getting started apply to meaningful conversation where you really just want to have fun talking to each other. The most common mistake people make is to think that the secret to good conversation is to be interesting. It's not. The secret is not to have interesting things to say, but *to be interested,* genuinely interested, in the person you're talking to and to show it.

Suggestion 3   Drawing Your Partner Out

People usually have a story to tell. That story is their story just like a painter portrays a scene in brush strokes that are special to that artist. People are like artists who see things in their own special ways. If you like someone, you will take delight in drawing out that person's own special way of reacting to and perceiving any event in life.

Encourage your spouse to talk about herself (himself). Try less to impress your spouse with how interesting and important you are. Rather, convey how interesting your partner is by taking pleasure in his (or her) stories and by being interested in aspects of your partner's experience that relate to you.

Suggestion 4   Talking About Your Partner's Interests

The royal road to a person's heart is talk about the things that that person treasures most. But to be able to do that you need to know about the person. What things are of major concern to this person? What are this person's chief delights? Interests?

If you talk to people in terms of *their* interests, you will be enriched by it. Remember also that two different people approaching the same interest or hobby will actually have totally different experiences with it. One person will enjoy boating for the peacefulness of it and another for the excitement. Try to find out about your spouse's special experience with his or her interests. And don't be satisfied with just a list of interests.

Suggestion 5   Reciprocating and Associating

If you followed Suggestions 3 and 4, you would be acting more like an interviewer than a friend. Conversation needs to be a two-sided adventure. You need to share your own experience as well as drawing the other person out. In this way you will be *reciprocating* in the conversation.

One way to do that is *to associate.* As the other person speaks, you will find that things that are being said remind you of things in your own life, or they make you think of related incidents that you want to share. Feel free to share these thoughts since they can enhance the flow of ideas between you.

It is OK to associate with something the other person is saying even if it means introducing a new topic.

Suggestion 6   Empathizing and Validating

As you listen try to put yourself in your spouse's shoes, and try to see things the way your spouse is seeing them. You can then say things that show you see how valid this point of view is. This is called "validating." Statements that validate also communicate that you think it makes sense or is legitimate to act, feel, and think things the way the other person does. For example, "Yeah, that must have hurt your feelings," or "That would have made me mad too," or "I know just what you're going through."

After you use Suggestion 6, follow it with Suggestion 5. After validating, you can lead in to an association of your own. For example, "I know just what you mean. My boss gets me mad by doing the same thing."

Suggestion 7   Paraphrasing and Checking Perceptions

In order to find out if you are tuned in, try to summarize, in your own words, what you think the other person is saying. You can use either a question or a statement. Try starting your paraphrase with:

> "So what you're saying is. . ." or
> "What you've said so far is . . ." or
> "What I understand is that . . . ."

Ending and follow-up. When you want to end a conversation, the best thing to do is to be direct about it, and to leave no doubt in your spouse's mind about why you are stopping. You might simply say "Excuse me, I've enjoyed talking, but I've got to run or I'll be late." If you want to, you can mention getting together again at a specific time later. Also, try to be sensitive to your spouse's need to stop talking and make it easy for him or her to take leave of you. Follow-up is important when you next meet. Try to develop a memory for those things you know about your spouse and those things you have shared. You can refer to the things you know and remember. And it will also show that you cared enough to remember.

Getting caught up with each other. An important time for most couples is coming together at the end of a day. It is also an appropriate time to be a good, active listener. This end-of-day catch up is somewhat like a news report. First we hear from "reporter No. 1," then from "reporter No. 2," although it can also go beyond mere reporting if you are both active listeners. If you listen well and ask questions, draw your partner out, reciprocate, associate, empathize, and validate, you will find that sharing the events of the day will draw you closer together, and you will start looking forward to sharing these moments with your spouse. So make time daily to get caught up with each other.

How to Have More Joy In Your Relationship

Getting started. Couples tend to get stuck in routine ways of living together. They do the same things every day. There are some variations, but even the variations soon become routine. Because they know just about everything there is to know about each other, many couples feel that there is no further excitement to look forward to. And it's easy to fall into patterns. All couples do it, but the trick is to be able to get unstuck once in a while and do fun things together. There's no limit to the enjoyable experiences couples can have once they decide to leave the safety of their day-to-day patterns.

THE FUN DECK

The Fun Deck is a deck of cards that you will create by cutting apart Appendix E of this book. Each card contains some activity that some couple said was fun for them. If you both look through the Fun Deck, you may find things to do together that you never thought of, or something you used to but no longer do. You can also use it to reminisce or to plan.

In addition to finding activities that would be fun to do together, you may get some ideas for doing things you'd like to do without your spouse. Intimacy does not mean an intense togetherness all the time. Doing some activities you enjoy on your own in the long run may also enhance intimacy when you do get together.

Some Suggestions for Fun

There is no magic wand which you can wave and "presto" more joy will enter your life. You have to *create* joyful experiences for each other. But any couple is capable of having more joy in their relationship. Below are a few basic suggestions that should help.

Suggestion 1   Brainstorm

Ask yourself "What are the most interesting, enjoyable, fun things that we do with each other." Let your imagination and experience be your guide. When you brainstorm, consider all your ideas, no matter how foolish they sound; you never know—the most foolish ideas just might be the most fun. The rule in brainstorming is: never be negative about any suggestion (no matter how dumb it seems).

Suggestion 2   Collaborate

Talk to each other about the experiences that you think will be fun for both of you, and then decide which fun experiences you will try.

Suggestion 3   Do it!

Many of the world's greatest ideas remain ideas because they are never put into action. Once you decide to try a fun experience, don't wait, *do it now* or at least set aside a time when you will do it.

Below is an example of two types of couples. One couple is stuck in their everyday pattern of living, while the other couple creates fun experiences for themselves. See if you can tell the couples apart.

Couple No. 1:

Mary: Wouldn't it be fun to drive to the city and have some Dutch apple crumb donuts.

Harry: Yes, but it's a long drive. We can go some other time.

Mary: Well, I guess you're right.

Harry: Let's turn on the TV.

Couple No. 2:

Mary: Wouldn't it be fun to drive to the city and have some Dutch apple crumb donuts.

Harry: Great idea, Mary. I'd really love to have a good donut to-night. It's a long drive, but it will be fun talking as we go.

Mary: Good! Let's go. I guess I'll have to miss the Mary Tyler Moore show tonight. But who cares—this'll be fun.

153

Suggestion 4   Experiment

Try new ideas, you have nothing to lose—joy to gain! Think about what you do during each week. *What one thing would you want to do that would be joy producing for you?* Once you have answered this question, find a way to include some of that activity into each week. If you have to cancel or postpone other activities, or change priorities in your life, then do so.

Some Enjoyable Sensual Experiences to Try

Pleasuring. Making each other feel better will probably make you feel closer to each other. Nondemand pleasuring is a form of sensual touching and massage where there is no demand for, or expectation of, sexual intercourse. Even though it has been used in sexual counseling, even with a good relationship an evening of pleasuring can be an enjoyable break from routine and a fun reintroduction to each other's bodies. For these experiences you should put aside a large block of time (about one to two hours minimum) and choose a comfortable place like your bedroom or, for some adventurous couples, a local motel or hotel. Also buy some hand or face lotion. Physician's Formula Emollient Oil (nonallergenic) is good.

The basic idea behind caressing each other is very simple: It's nice to feel good. The person who is caressing is the giver. The one who receives the caress is the receiver. Below are a few suggestions which, if followed, will help make the caressing as enjoyable as possible.

Suggestion 1   Decide Who Will Be the Giver and Receiver

It is important when receiving pleasure that you do not worry about giving pleasure. In a pleasuring experience one person gives and the other receives. Try to follow the example of the cat being petted—the cat is totally absorbed, concentrating only on its own sensation.

Suggestion 2   Tell Each Other How You Like
to Be Caressed

Many couples do not share with each other what feels

good to them. In order for your spouse to make you feel good, he (she) has to know what makes you feel good. So let your partner know how you like to be kissed, fondled, held. Talk to each other about what you want the other person to do for you.

Suggestion 3   Show Your Spouse What You Want
It's a good idea to show your spouse what feels good. Move your spouse's hands the way you want them to move.

Suggestion 4   Please Each Other
Take this opportunity to learn about your spouse. You may find that many of the expectations you have about what feels good to your spouse are wrong.

Suggestion 5   Be As Tender and Sensitive as Possible to Each Other's Needs
Don't be defensive as you learn about what does and doesn't feel good to your spouse. What you learn says nothing about your own adequacy—every person has a unique set of tastes in receiving pleasure.

Suggestion 6   Follow Each Other's Suggestions
Try to be as open and receptive to your spouse's comments as possible. Remember he or she knows best what feels good. Remember also that being told to try something else does not mean that your spouse is rejecting you as a lover. It means that there are ways to make your partner feel even better.

Suggestion 7   Ask Simple Questions
During the caressing, the giver should ask the receiver questions such as:

How are you feeling?

Are you enjoying this?

Do you want it higher, lower, harder, softer, faster, slower . . .?

This is important for two reasons. It makes it easier for the receiver to just say yes or no rather than to have to ask you to do this or that; and it allows you to get immediate feedback about the effect of caresses that you give your spouse.

Suggestion 8   If It Feels Good, Take the Time
to Fully Enjoy It
In other words, take your time and do the caressing slowly. Devote your full attention to what you are doing and how your spouse is feeling.

Suggestion 9   Enjoy Both the Giving and the Receiving
Enjoy the feeling that your spouse is giving you while you are being caressed. You will have a turn to give pleasure to your spouse, so relax and let your body react to the tender touches.

As you go through these pleasurable experiences, remember the nine suggestions for enjoyable caressing.

Summary
1. Decide who will be the giver and receiver.
2. Tell each other how you like to be caressed.
3. Show your spouse what you want.
4. Please each other.
5. Be as tender and sensitive as possible to each other's needs.
6. Follow each other's suggestions.
7. Ask simple questions.
8. If it feels good, take the time to fully enjoy it.
9. Enjoy both the giving and the receiving.

The Good-by—Hello Experience
Quietly sit down and shut your eyes. Imagine that you will never see each other again and that you are about to say good-by for the last time. Let your emotions build up as you think about saying good-by. Then, with your eyes still closed, starting with only your hands, say good-by to your spouse. Don't use words—only your hands. Then *slowly* use other parts of your body to say good-by to your spouse nonverbally. You can hold, touch, kiss, etc. Remember to take your time and use your caresses to communicate your feelings to each other. Then after you

"part," sit down again and imagine that you will be seeing each other for the first time after a terribly long time apart. Let your emotions build up as you think about saying "hello" to each other after the long separation. Then with your eyes still closed, use only your hands to say hello to your spouse. Then *slowly* use other parts of your body to caress each other as you communicate the joy you feel in seeing one another again.

After the good-by experience, talk about how each of you felt, what felt particularly good, and what each of you could have done to make the experience feel even better.

Foot caress experiences. First decide who will be the giver and the receiver. The giver, using an agreeable hand lotion or baby oil, *slowly* caresses the receiver's foot. Remember the "Suggestions for Pleasuring."

Facial caress. The giver, using an agreeable face cream, slowly explores and caresses the receiver's face. During the experience, let the receiver show the giver how he or she likes to have the face caressed by placing the receiver's hand over the giver's hand and moving it as the receiver desires. Remember the suggestions for enjoyable caresses and talk about the experience when you are finished.

Body caress. The receiver lies face down. The giver, again using an agreeable body lotion, starts with the receiver's back and *slowly* caresses the whole body. Then the receiver turns over and the front is slowly caressed. In this experience no special attention is given to the breasts or genitals.

Sexual caress. This experience follows the body caress. Using a special nonallergenic oil (Physician's Formula Emollient Oil) the giver pays special attention to the receiver's genitals and breasts. Remember to follow the suggestions: Go slow, ask for and give feedback.

Sharing fantasies. It is sad that we adults rarely stray from the world of the practical where we worry about hard reality. We rarely take the time to play together with our

157

imaginations. When we take time off, we seek entertainment in which we watch the products of other people's imagination.

This may sound silly to you, but some of the closest experiences couples have occur very rarely, and they seem to occur when they talk about the impossible, the fantastic, when they build that impossible castle on top of a mountain instead of discussing repairing some leaky pipes. Or when they take a makebelieve, pretend trip while they are actually sitting in their living room with the lights off.

We'd like to suggest some "directed fantasies" for you. When you try these, one of you can start reading the fantasy while the other has his or her eyes closed. Then both of you can start experiencing and suggesting things to imagine. This is like a round-robin story where one person starts the story, and the story goes around a circle of people. Except here there are just the two of you. Start your fantasy experience by turning down the lights. Close your eyes, relax, and get comfortable; take your time. One of you begin by suggesting a fantasy. Think, "Where would I like to be?" or "What would I like to be?" or "Who would I like to be?" or "What would I like to be doing?" (Example: I am exploring a moon of Mars. The atmosphere is sweet. I am going down a deserted road to what appears to be a lost civilization.)

The other person should accept this start and build on it. (Example: Up ahead there is a city encased in a glass bubble. It has golden turrets.)

Now go along together, building the fantasy and sharing what you imagine. Below are some other suggestions for fantasies you can use. After a while you can make up your own and totally use your own imagination.

1. You are hiking up a mountainside. It is a beautiful day. The sky clouds over. As it begins to rain you see a cave. You hesitate and then go in. Explore the cave. What do you see there? As you walk along in the cave you see a passageway. You follow it. There is a light up ahead.

2. Imagine yourself becoming very small in your own home. You are wandering around and find yourself able to walk on the walls. As you sit on a picture in your home you see yourself sitting. You regard your body from outside yourself.
3. You are walking along a path. You take all the things that are making you tense, the things you are worried about, and you put them all in a box. Then you throw the box far away. A weight has been lifted from you. The place is a familiar spot, someplace you'd like to be. Explore this place. Walk on. Find something special. Look at it, feel it, appreciate it.

Additional information on sharing fantasies can be found in Herbert Otto's book, *Fantasy Encounter Games* (Wilshire Book Co., 1974).

Sharing dreams. With a little practice, many people have learned to remember their dreams. Interest in dreams is as old as the Biblical story of Joseph's interpretation of the Pharaoh's dream. In that case Joseph interpreted the dreams in terms of signs of real events to come. But there are other ways to interpret dreams. Events in dreams may be wishes or fears. Each character in a dream may be a part of the dreamer, an aspect of the dreamer's personality. You may find it an important experience to share each other's dreams.

Relaxation. One of the things that each of you will benefit from is learning how to relax. Make some time together when one of you helps the other to relax. Teach each other to relax by first tensing and then relaxing your various muscles. If you are working with a therapist, we recommend *Progressive Relaxation Training* by Bernstein and Borkovec (Research Press, 1973).

Sensation. Get a copy of *Sense Relaxation Below Your Mind* by Bernard Gunther (Macmillan, Inc., 1968). It suggests exercises to heighten your experience of sensation alone and with your partner.

Massage. Get a copy of the *Massage Book* by George Downing (Random House, 1972) to learn how to give each other a good massage.

Exploring sexuality. Get a copy of the *Joy of Sex* edited by Alex Comfort (Crown Publishing, Inc., 1972).

9 GETTING OUT OF A BAD MARRIAGE

This chapter is based primarily on our clinical experience with distressed couples who went through the decision to get a divorce, and on research on divorce. Since there are few facts and much speculation in this area, much of what we say may be biased by our own values. Thus we offer our recommendations and suggestions modestly. Our intention is to provide you with enough information and suggestions so that you can make good problem-solving decisions during this difficult time. This chapter may also help you decide whether or not you want to continue your relationship. If you decide to separate or divorce, these guidelines may help you end the marriage in a way that is best for all concerned.

CONSIDERING DIVORCE AND SEPARATION

Couples confront the issue of divorce or separation for many reasons. Whatever the reasons, most couples report having to face a number of common issues, and these issues are best dealt with in an open and honest way. Before exploring these issues, however, it is important to realize that frequently one spouse wants out of the marriage more than the other, or that sometimes one spouse does not want to face the possibility of divorce or separation, and the other must face the issues alone. We are not suggesting that you can keep pain out of the experience, or that we can help you to see it as a happy event. For most people it is an extremely difficult life experience. However, we do have a few goals to suggest.

161

The first goal is to manage the process so that it is not destructive to either of you, and so that you do not devalue yourselves. Our second goal involves those couples with children. The goal is to continue being able to be good parents even if you cannot remain a couple. This involves not using the children as a political football in your own relationship. We will recommend some guidelines and exercises to help you accomplish these goals. We will also recommend some books for you to read that may help.

GUIDELINES FOR CONSIDERING DIVORCE

Take Your Time Making the Decision
You have probably been together for a long time, so there is no need to rush into a decision to divorce. Take the time and make the effort to consider these guidelines before making a decision.

Continue Using the Communication Skills
As You Discuss the Possibility of Divorce
Since the topic of divorce is bound to be very emotional and anxiety-producing, good communication will be difficult to maintain. However, it is at this time that good communication is essential. Particularly important is the use of leveling (Chapter 2) and the ability to recognize and deal with hidden agendas (Chapter 5). These skills will help you to lay all your cards on the table so that you and your spouse know what is involved before making a decision. Further, the crisis chapter (Chapter 7) will help you at times of great emotional stress, and stress can be expected during this period.

Set Aside Time to Discuss the Divorce Issue
When the possibility of divorce or separation is first mentioned, you and your spouse will likely experience complex emotional reactions. Feelings of rejection, threat, insecurity, fear, hopelessness, freedom, guilt, loneliness, and depression may dominate your consciousness. It is important for these feelings to be communicated so that you

both can get an idea of where you stand, what you feel, and what you think. One way to accomplish this goal is to schedule a meeting so that you can talk with no external pressures. After the first meeting, you can set up a time for another meeting. Planning another meeting may provide a structure which helps reduce the pain and confusion commonly experienced by couples going through the crisis of talking about divorce.

Recognize and Accept the Pain
You and Your Spouse Are Feeling
Consideration of divorce will probably be very difficult and painful for you and your spouse. These feelings are natural responses to a difficult situation. Try to express your pain by leveling, and try to support your spouse's feelings by validating.

Be Prepared for Feelings of Ambivalence
Jan Fuller (1973) wrote a book about her divorce. In it she describes her reactions to situations which many divorced people encounter. Concerning ambivalence she writes: "During my marriage, I both loved and hated E. H., and this still holds true. . . . I wanted both the marriage and the divorce . . . . *Ambivalence* is an emotion I most genuinely feel" (p. 29, emphasis ours). Most people we have seen who have been considering divorce or separation are not really sure whether they want to leave or to stay. If your spouse is the one who most wants to leave, you might expect some wavering back and forth as to what he or she really wants. If this is the case, you have the right to decide how you want to deal with your spouse's ambivalence. If you feel you can't live in such an uncertain situation, then perhaps a temporary separation is in order (see below for discussion of separations). However, if you decide to stay with an ambivalent partner, you are then accepting the responsibility for what you will experience.

Confront Your Catastrophic Expectations About Divorce
Fuller (1973) writes about her own experiences: "My values are changing. Things I once assumed to be true I

now question . . . . All that is important to me is that my beliefs keep pace with my behavior, and my behavior reflects my beliefs, and that both are subject to change whenever change seems in order" (p. 101). There are two sources of catastrophic expectations concerning divorce. One from the societal myths about divorce, and the other from your own perceptions and fears about divorce.

Myths about divorce. There are many popular myths about divorce. Below are several along with a rational explication of each.

1. *You should stay together for your children.* There was a time when distressed couples accepted this statement as a truth, and consequently suffered through many years of unhappiness. Now this belief has been challenged by common sense and by published research, both of which suggest that there is no easy answer to the question of the effects of divorce on children. Clearly, divorce will have some impact on the children; however, so will growing up in a distressed family situation. It is important for you to decide to divorce or not to on the basis of the facts of the situation, and not just because you think it is best for the children. Even though research reports are contradictory, we can conclude that it may be worse for the children to grow up in a distressed two-parent family as opposed to a warm and loving one-parent family.

2. *Divorce is a cop-out.* This myth suggests that people who want a divorce are looking for an easy way out of marital difficulties. Quite to the contrary, most couples who divorce have exhausted alternatives within the marriage and consider divorce as a last resort. Furthermore, divorce is certainly not an "easy" experience for anyone; going through a divorce is a difficult, trying, but hopefully a constructive experience. In other words, to divorce takes courage; it is not a cop-out.

3. *Divorce is a destructive experience.* Divorce is neither good nor bad. How the individual handles the divorce determines the impact on his or her life. Many people believe that divorce is by definition a negative experience. We disagree. Some couples just aren't right for each other, and divorce can lead to new opportunities for independence and growth for people who were stuck in unhappy, conflict-ridden, or dead marriages.

Personal catastrophic expectations. In order for you to get in touch with your own personal catastrophic expectations, take some time to consider your beliefs and perceptions about divorce and divorced people. Write these down and then determine whether or not they have any basis in reality. Discuss these feelings with your friends or spouse so that you can get a more realistic idea of your views.

Make Your Own Decisions and Avoid Psychopests

Most people are willing to give advice. When your friends and acquaintances learn of your situation, it is likely that you will get all sorts of counsel, some of it you asked for, some of it given without your permission. People who give advice or feedback without first being asked have been called "psychopests" (Schutz, 1958). Advice givers, psychopests or not, are usually biased, either due to personal involvement in the situation, or because of their own personal needs and problems. At this crucial time in your life, when you are considering divorce, you will probably find yourself wanting someone to tell you what to do, and such people can usually be found. We feel that friends and acquaintances can be most helpful just by listening to you—by supporting and validiating *your* feelings. However, since *you* are the one who must experience and take responsibility for the consequences of the decision, *you* are the one who should make these decisions. If you feel your friends and acquaintances are not completely meeting your needs, you have the option of consultation with an uninvolved professional, a psychologist or a marriage counselor.

Don't Lie to Your Children About Obvious Conflicts

Even if you do not tell your children that something is wrong with your marriage, they will know. Children are perceptive of nonverbal messages from their parents, and will sense that something is wrong. We do not, however, recommend that you tell your children that you are considering divorce. There is no need to create ambiguity for them. Rather, you can communicate to them, using your own style, that "Mommy and Daddy are having some problems and are trying to work things out." As we will mention later on in this chapter, it is important for you to communicate to your children that they are not to blame for marital conflicts, and that you love them. Children may blame themselves for your problems, and this belief will create further problems for the family if it is not clarified. We recommend Desport's *Children of Divorce* (1962) for couples interested in further reading about the impact of divorce on children, and for further advice on communicating with your children.

ALTERNATIVES TO DIVORCE

Below are a few possible alternatives to divorce which are available to distressed couples who are considering divorce.

Deciding to Work on Problems in the Relationship

This involves a renewal of efforts to solve problems in the relationship. Couples who choose this alternative probably have decided that their problems are solvable and have the motivation to try to solve them. Some professional assistance may be very helpful to couples at this point, especially to couples who have previously been unsuccessful at solving problems on their own.

Declaring A Moratorium

This involves deciding to postpone the decision to divorce, and to try something else. For instance, a couple may decide that the wife will go to work part-time, and that the husband will take care of the children two days a week. They declare a moratorium on discussions about divorce for a month while they try out this new situation. We recommend that couples declaring a moratorium use Chapter 4 (Negotiating Agreements) to help work out a concrete, mutually acceptable plan.

Separation

For many couples, separation is the step before divorce. Many issues come up for couples who decide to separate. These include splitting up possessions, where to live, seeing other people (and deciding what that means), conditions for getting back together, and so on. Because of the complexities involved in negotiating a workable separation, we suggest using Chapter 4 to help you write out a specific separation agreement. It is important to include a provision for changing the agreement if the need arises. For instance, if you agree to separate for two months, and then one of you wants more time, then the original separation agreement should be reconsidered and revised according to the new situation.

HAVING A CONSTRUCTIVE DIVORCE

This part of the chapter is written for couples who have decided to divorce.

Divorce is traditionally viewed as a painful, destructive experience for both parents and children. We see no way of helping you avoid the pain associated with marital breakup. However, the divorce experience does not have to be destructive. We view divorce itself as neither positive nor negative. The way you handle the divorce determines the impact it has on you. Getting a divorce is a statement that the relationship did not work out; it is not a statement about the worth of the people involved. Many divorced people make the mistake of blaming themselves or their spouses (for example, "I'm a rotten person"; "He's a rotten person"). A more useful explanation of why the marriage broke up is that the relationship was not satisfying to both partners, or that the two people did not mesh together very well. We choose to look at the cause of marital distress and divorce as problems in the relationship. If you look at the causes of divorce in those terms, and you don't blame yourself, it may help you face divorce in a constructive way.

Just as a glass of water can be viewed as half full or half empty, divorce also can be viewed in two ways. One way is to view divorce as continued misery, and the other way is to think of divorce as an opportunity for creating a more satisfying, fulfilling, joyful life. We recommend the second perspective and hope you will adopt this way of looking at the future. It may help to present common problems faced by people like yourself, and to suggest some ways to solve these problems. The feelings and problems you are experiencing are probably not unique to you, even though they may seem so right now. The best way to find this out for yourself is to talk to other people who either are going through a divorce, or who have recently done so. Another alternative is to read some personal accounts of divorce which are available. Two books we recommend are: *Creative Divorce* (Krantzler, 1974; a male perspective) and Jan Fuller's *Space* (quoted above).

There are two major types of problems: the practical and the social and psychological. We will first discuss the practical, then the social and psychological problems.

Legal Aspects
Since marriage is a legal as well as a social institution, dissolution of a marriage entails legal action. Divorce differs from state to state, and the legal process is rapidly changing.

The concept of a "no fault" divorce is becoming increasingly popular and relevant, and if both partners want a divorce, this alternative might be considered with the help of a lawyer. Since we do not pretend to be legal experts, we recommend you consult an attorney or legal aid society to help you with these aspects of divorce. There are also a number of books available which cover legal problems associated with divorce (Wheeler, 1975; Baskin & Kiel-Friedman, 1974; Mayer, 1971).

Children

Traditionally the wife has been awarded the custody of the children; however, there has recently been more social acceptance of fathers raising their children. Deciding who should get custody of the children is a couple's problem, and we can offer no easy solutions. However, we can suggest some things to consider when making the decision. First, do you want the responsibility and challenge of raising the children? It is important *to level* with yourself and each other so that you can make your decision based on what you want to do versus what you think you *should* do.

Second, who can provide the best home for the children? For example, do you have a job which requires travel, and consequently takes time away from home and the children? *The most important consideration here is the welfare of the children.*

Third, what do your children have to say? If they are old enough, they may have valid reasons for living with one particular parent. Listen to what they have to say.

Finally, we want to point out that the ultimate decision maker in the case of children is the judge, so it is important for you or your lawyer to communicate the results of your decision or deliberations to the judge.

Visitation

Visitation rights will be part of the overall divorce agreement. We feel that it is important for the children to have the right to spend time with the out-of-house parent. However, since the shift from one parent to the other will tend to be difficult, at least initially, we recommend that structured times be set up and adhered to in order to help the children adjust to this new state of affairs.

Living Arrangements

At least one person will be changing his or her home. When former spouses live in the same community, they inevitably run into each other. This is caused by simple proximity as well as shared social networks. For many people, repeated interaction with their "ex" is painful and distressing. In these cases, it is advisable to try to live in different communities, if at all possible, so that interaction can occur at planned times, such as when the out-of-house parent comes to pick up the children. Further discussion of relations with your former spouse will be pursued later in this chapter.

SOCIAL AND PSYCHOLOGICAL PROBLEMS

The Feelings of Pain and Loneliness

These feelings are to be expected; trying to deny or avoid them will probably be unproductive. For example, Fuller (1973) writes "I used to value being cool . . . . Now I would rather show how hurt I can be. Better to be honest and let my vulnerability show" (p. 113). Confront these feelings, accept them and share them with friends. They will disappear with time, not because of time itself, although that will be part of it, but because of the new experiences and people you encounter during that time. Also, you might want to keep a journal of your thoughts and feelings about your divorce. This may help you to consider and express some of your inner experiences which are hard to communicate to others. For an example of such a journal, see Jan Fuller's book, *Space*. She writes, "The kids are at E. H.'s and it's Saturday night and I am alone. Really alone. Not just alone, lonely" (p. 50).

Relations With Former Spouse

There are two main feelings that people have toward relations with their former spouse. One is "Gee, I'd like to be friends with him or her"; and two, "I never want to see him or her again." If you read popular books on divorce, you will find arguments supporting both positions toward the "ex." We feel that it is unrealistic to expect to be great friends with your former spouse. For starters, there are emotional ties which have been severed, and psychological scar tissue takes time to develop. Time itself doesn't provide the substance of the "scar tissue." Rather, new experiences and new relationships help you to develop new emotional bonds, and allow old ones to change. Trying to be intimate with your former spouse will reopen wounds, and take energy away from other tasks confronting you at this time in your life.

Furthermore, you are probably setting yourself up for another disappointing and frustrating experience because the odds against maintaining a meaningful relationship with your "ex" are great. There is a pressure that many divorced people feel to be friends with their "ex," and it's almost like the "in" thing to do. We feel that it's important to consider the reasons for wanting to be friends, and then to decide what you think is best for you.

You may ask yourself at this time "What about the children? Isn't it important for us to be friends so that the children will benefit?" This is a complex issue, with no simple answer. It is more important for the children to be able to communicate with each of you than for each of you to be able to communicate with each other. As long as you and your "ex" can be polite to each other, and can communicate information about essential events (e.g., when the out-of-house parent is coming to visit), then that is sufficient. The children will benefit more from a meaningful relationship with each of their parents as separate individuals. If visitations become a time for former spouses to interact with each other, and not for the out-of-house parent to interact with the children, then the goal of a good relationship between parent and child is somewhat sacrificed.

In summary, we recommend that you strive to have a "polite" relationship with your "ex," not an intimate relationship. If a friendly relationship develops, and you feel that both of you can handle it, then that's fine.

What to Tell the Children
There are three important messages to communicate to your children. How you do so depends on your own style and the ages of the children. Message one involves telling them the facts of the situation. We recommend that you

171

be honest with your children and tell them something like, "Your father (mother) and I are not happy living together, and our feelings toward each other have changed, so we will be getting a divorce." This message informs the children that you will be getting a divorce and why you are getting a divorce. Including the why is important, and leads us into message two, which is that you should communicate to the children that the breakup is not due to them. To ensure that the children do not blame themselves, you might add, "We are breaking up because we no longer get along and we do not want to live together any more, but both of us love you and will continue to do so." This last statement communicates message three to the children—that you still love them, and that you will continue to love them.

A summary of the three messages to communicate to your children includes (1) the facts: you are divorcing and why; (2) you are to blame for the divorce and not the children; (3) you still love them and will continue to love them.

Child Rearing

Obviously the parent with whom the children live will have the primary responsibility for the day-to-day problems of child rearing. However, this does not mean that the out-of-house parent cannot be an influence. Problems with the children can be discussed at "parent meetings" designed specifically for the purpose of solving problems with the children. Such meetings are more appropriate for situations in which the out-of-house parent has frequent contact with the children.

If you or your former spouse has remarried, then we recommend that the out-of-house parent respect the parenting responsibilities of the step-father or step-mother in order to reduce confusion for the children. A common problem faced by many divorced parents is what to do about discrepancies in how the parents handle the children. There may be different "rules" for the children to follow in different households (for example, bedtime may be 9 p.m. in one home, 10 p.m. in the other). One way to help the children cope with rule differences is to communicate to them the meaning of the proverb, "When in Rome, do as the Romans do." The children can be taught to respect differences in their parents' life styles.

Remember, the children's welfare is the most important consideration when you are making decisions which involve them.

Social Roles and Social Life

You may be experiencing what sociologists call anomie or normlessness. Anomie involves feeling confused, bewildered, and insecure because you are not certain about how to act in social situations, and you are not sure how others expect you to be. This situation commonly exists for divorced people because there are no clearly defined rules for how to act with people. Thus you have great freedom to choose among a wide range of alternative ways of acting. In other words, you will be developing a new life style.

One solution to the problem of normlessness is for you to view yourself as a *single* rather than a divorced person. Then you will have a set of norms which may help you in social interactions.

The experience of changing your life style can be simultaneously threatening, scary, and exciting. For example Fuller (1973) writes "This is the first time in my life that I have the opportunity to be a free human being to come and go as I please, and I don't want to have to depend on anybody's whims" (p. 24); and "I find it strange taking on the role of divorcee, because I feel the only thing my children and I automatically have in common with other divorcees and their children is the way we are characterized. When will people learn that there is no shortcut to knowing another individual" (p. 83). We recommend that you adopt a perspective of experimentation; try new things, and find out what you like, what you dislike. For many, experimentation involves taking *risks.* In many situations you may feel very hesitant to try something new. For example, Fuller writes "Getting back to dating is not easy. I find that half the responsibility for reaching out and showing interest is mine, and unless I make this rather terrifying effort nothing much happens" (p. 56).

At these times it is useful to get in touch with your catastrophic expectations about the situation. One way is to become aware of what you say to yourself at these times. For instance, in the dating example you are considering asking person X out. You may be saying to yourself "X will never go out with me—I have nothing to offer X, and when he says 'No' I'll be really hurt." After you find out what you're saying to yourself, challenge the logic underlying the statements. In this case, you could say to yourself, "That's ridiculous. How do I know what X will say till I ask him? I have a lot to offer; I'm attractive, interesting, and fun to be with. Further, if X says 'No,' that's not the worst possible thing in the world; it's not my loss."

Risk taking involves experiencing some disappointments. It is important to learn from your disappointing experiences, and not to interpret them as failures, or as meaning you're a bad or worthless person. Keep in mind the "Babe Ruth Theory of Interaction." This theory follows from the fact that Babe Ruth hit more home runs than anyone. Everyone knows this. However, few people realize that Babe Ruth, besides being a home run king, was also a strike out king. He had the second most strike outs during a career. The moral of the story is that in order to hit home runs, you must occasionally strike out!

Relating To Others

Many people may ask you questions which make you feel uncomfortable. There is no reason for you to answer questions which you do not want to answer. Jan Fuller (1973) handles this situation as follows: "When . . . somebody asks me, 'Don't you think it's better for the children if couples stay together?' I reply 'I imagine you feel that married people should stay together if possible.' This enables the other person to express his views without demanding that I agree or disagree" (p. 17). Other questions like "Why did you get a divorce?" can just go unanswered, or you can say that you'd prefer not to talk about it right now.

Many divorced people are used to relating to people as a couple and find it difficult to be an "I" instead of a "We." You may even notice yourself saying "We feel" instead of "I feel" during conversations. Jan Fuller writes "I am beginning to have a sense of myself in my new identity. From the 'half-person' I felt in my marriage, I am now beginning to fill in that other half, not with another person, but with myself" (p. 99). Recently divorced people face the common tasks of (1) relating to old friends and acquaintances as a single person rather than a married person who is part of a couple, and (2) meeting new people and making new friends. The communication skills you learned in the previous chapters of this book can be used to help you with these tasks. If you find you are having trouble relating to people, take a refresher course on the use of communication skills by rereading parts of the book which you feel are relevant for the problems you are encountering. For instance, if you are having trouble with the initial stages of forming a relationship, practice your listening and validating skills (Chapter 1). If your relationships with old friends seem superficial, try leveling more (Chapter 2), or look for hidden agendas (Chapter 5).

APPENDIXES

The following appendixes include a Problem Inventory for the Husband and Wife, a Knowledge Assessment Self-Test, a Troubleshooting Guide and an Up Deck and Fun Deck.

APPENDIX A
HUSBAND'S PROBLEM INVENTORY

Name _____

Date _____

Instructions. On page 179 is a list of areas of disagreement experienced by many couples. Use this inventory to decide on a problem (see page 5, Chapter 1).

In the first column please indicate how severe the problem is by placing a number from 0 to 100. A zero indicates that the problem is not severe, and a 100 indicates that it is a very severe problem area.

In the second column, please write the number of years, months, weeks, or days that this area has been a problem.

For example:

	How severe?	How long?
Alcohol and drugs	90	2½ yr.

This indicates that alcohol and drugs are in your opinion a serious problem and that it has been a problem for about 2½ years.

	How severe?	How long?
1. Money		
2. Communication		
3. In-laws		
4. Sex		
5. Religion		
6. Recreation		
7. Friends		
8. Alcohol and Drugs		
9. Children		
10. Jealousy		

Please feel free to write down any other problem area(s) which you may feel is (are) relevant.

11.		
12.		

WIFE'S PROBLEM INVENTORY

Name _____

Date _____

Instructions. On page 181 is a list of areas of disagreement experienced by many couples. Use this inventory to decide on a problem (see page 5, Chapter 1).

In the first column please indicate how severe the problem is by placing a number from 0 to 100. A zero indicates that the problem is not severe and a 100 indicates that it is a very severe problem area.

In the second column, please write the number of years, months, weeks, or days that this area has been a problem.

For example:

	How severe?	How long?
Alcohol and drugs	90	2½ yr.

This indicates that alcohol and drugs are in your opinion a serious problem and that it has been a problem for about 2½ years.

	How severe?	How long?
1. Money		
2. Communication		
3. In-laws		
4. Sex		
5. Religion		
6. Recreation		
7. Friends		
8. Alcohol and Drugs		
9. Children		
10. Jelousy		

Please feel free to write down any other problem area(s) which you may feel is (are) relevant.

11.		
12.		

APPENDIX B
KNOWLEDGE ASSESSMENT SELF-TEST

1. Define good communication using *Intent* and *Impact:*

2. A basic problem of not listening is the _____
   _____
   _____ Syndrome.

3. Define *feedback:*

4. When a conversation seems to be getting out of hand,
   and you have the feeling that Intents do not match
   Impacts, you should call a S_____ A_____.

5. What are two parts of any message?

 a. _____

 b. _____

6. How can you end a *Standoff?*

7. Define *validating?*

8. Match the problem on the left with the correct intervention on the right.

 ___Not listening   a. Validation
 ___Cross complaining   b. Check out and paraphrase
 ___Standoff   c. Make an agenda
 ___Nondecisions   d. Ritualize decision making process

9. What is the best way to make leveling statements?

10. Define the following:

    a. Kitchen sinking:

    b. Character assassination:

    c. Yes—butting:

    d. Mind reading:

    e. Off beam:

11. How do you end the SS Syndrome?

12. What is the Feeling Chart and how do you use it?

13. Take these negative nebulous statements and make them positive specific suggestions for change:

a. "You don't care about me."

b. "You're irresponsible."

c. "You act so superior."

14. What is the basic idea of editing and politeness?

15. What is a *hidden agenda?*

16. Name the three kinds of hidden agendas:

17. How can you tell when a couple has a hidden agenda?

18. How do you deal with a hidden agenda?

19. What are the three parts of a Family Meeting?

g _____ time

a _____ b _____ time

p _____ s _____ time

20. What is the Up Deck?

21. How do you negotiate a contract using the Up Deck?

22. What is the Fun Deck?

23. List as many of the nine rules of politeness as you can.

APPENDIX C
TROUBLESHOOTING GUIDE

Problem	*Intervention*
1. Intent/Impact discrepancy	Listening: Check-out and paraphrase. Use Stop Action and the Floor with Impact cards.
2. One spouse feels put down	Validation.
3. Off Beam	Stop Action; back On Beam.
4. Mind Reading	Ask how spouse *feels*.
5. Kitchen sinking; Cross-complaining	Stop Action; Make an agenda; pick one issue at a time.
6. Yes—butting; Summarizing Self Syndrome	Check-out, paraphrase, validate.
7. Standoff	Say, "What can we do to make things better?" "Here's what I would be willing to do to make things better."
8. Nondecisions	Make a written contract; post it in a public place.
9. Don't know what you're feeling	Use the Feeling Chart, Chapter 2, p. 32.
10. Can't deal too well with spouse's feeling	Suggestion Box.
11. Can't request behavior change	Assertion, Chapter 2, p. 33.

187

Problem	Intervention
12. Can't level	Make statements, "When you do X in situation Y I feel Z."
13. Character assassination Insults	Talk in terms of what spouse *does*, specifically. *Be* specific. "X Y Z Statements."
14. Feel out of touch with spouse	Schedule a "date" to get back in touch.
15. Ignoring each other	Each day have a time to share events of day.
16. Being rude	Institute a Politeness Week. Use etiquette rules in Chapter 7.
17. Feeling put down	See the Nine Rules of Politeness (p. 47)
18. Family Meetings don't go well	Have three parts to Family Meeting: Gripe Time, Agenda Building, Problem Solving.
19. Can't negotiate agreements	Contracting
a. Too negative	a. Nebulous Negative—Positive Specific Exercise, p. 79.
b. How to make things better	b. Use Up Deck. Write a contract.
c. Can't implement agreement	c. See Self-change exercise, Chapter 4, p. 71.
d. Rewards get fouled up	d. Your rewards should not be at a high cost to spouse.
e. Other problems	e. Are you being Positive? Specific?
20. Spinning wheels	Is there a hidden agenda?

APPENDIX D
THE UP DECK

Instructions: These cards contain suggestions of things that can bring you or your spouse "up." To make using the Up Deck easier, take a pair of scissors and cut out the individual cards to form a deck.

Getting a household repair done	Balancing the checkbook	Preparing an entire meal
Paying a bill	Helping with dinner	Doing some needed gardening
Taking care of the car	Doing the dishes	Doing some shopping for things we need
Cleaning or straightening up a bit	Doing the laundry	Mending my clothes
Doing an errand	Mowing the lawn	Taking out the garbage
Setting the alarm clock	Feeding or taking care of the pets	Putting the children to bed

Giving the kids a chore to do	Helping with a fight between the kids	Having an enjoyable conversation
Taking care of the kids while I am busy	Getting a babysitter	Telling me something confidential
Making some extra money	Starting a conversation with me	Summarizing my point of view so I know he/she is listening
Giving a child a bath	Asking me how I feel	Doing something I ask
Spending time with the kids	Answering child's question	Forgiving me for something
Helping kids with school work	Helping to dress the children	Asking for my opinion

Trying to see my point of view when we're fighting	Sharing feelings or thoughts with me	Accepting modification of own point of view by including my opinions
Wishing me a good day	Being nice to me when we're with other people	Calming me down when I'm having a blow up
Laughing, chuckling, or smiling together about something	Asking me what I think about something	Being nice when I make a mistake
Listening to my problems with understanding	Thanking me for something I did	Answering my questions with respect
Asking me about my day	Agreeing with something I said	Apologizing to me
Saying that he/she likes something I did	Asking me questions to understand and show interest in something I said	Being patient or understanding with me when I'm being nasty or irritable

Giving me a nice greeting when we meet after being apart	Smiling at me or laughing with me	Giving me a massage or rubdown
Talking to me when I ask for some attention	Being nice to my friends	Initiating sex
Trying to cheer me up	Paying me a compliment	Touching me affectionately
Being nice even though I was mean	Looking nice (dress, shaving, etc.)	Hugging or kissing me
Praising me for something I did	Making one of my favorite foods	Responding to my sexual advances
Bringing me a present	Cuddling up to me	Doing something sexual that I really like

Letting me know that sex was enjoyable	Talking together about finances to help us stick to the budget	Talking about friends or relatives
Shopping for something together	Going out to dinner, movie, or a tavern	
Talking together about making a purchase	Playing sports together (tennis, baseball, etc.)	
Spending time together having fun	Playing games together (cards, board games, etc.)	
Planning or helping me to plan a social event	Suggesting something fun for us to do together	
Doing something together in the evening (watching TV, reading, etc.)	Playing with the kids together	

APPENDIX E
THE FUN DECK

Instructions: These cards contain a number of activities that other couples have found to be fun. Use them to help plan out some fun time together. Take a pair of scissors and cut out the individual cards to form a deck.

Going bicycle riding before Sunday breakfast	Gardening	Go on errands together—waste an hour or two driving around, going into different stores to get things
Taking dancing lessons	Visiting with friends	Playing games together or with friends (Scrabble, Monopoly, chess, etc.)
Camping	Playing frisbee	Taking a shower or bath together
Going to a carnival	Playing pool	Making donuts
Taking the family to the zoo or a museum	Treating ourselves to a big breakfast of pancakes, eggs, bacon, orange juice, toast	Daydreaming about a fantastic vacation you know you can't afford
Cross country skiing	Playing bridge with another couple	Going to an art museum or gallery

Starting an aquarium	Going to a concert	Renting a rowboat or canoe for the afternoon
Going sailing	Going to a ball game or other athletic event (basketball, football, hockey, swim meet)	Discussing politics
Writing letters to friends	Playing music together, (guitar, piano, banjo, etc.)	Playing tennis together
Going skating	Jogging	Doing funny skits and recording them on tape. Playing them back and laughing
Playing charades	Going window shopping together	Making wine together
Going bowling	Reading a play out loud	Playing golf (or miniature golf) together

Doing ''sense'' relaxation or meditating together	Just sitting around with the lights low and talk	Reading the Sunday paper together
Going to the race track	Playing cards	Going to the botanical gardens
Stargazing when it gets warm, lying on your back and learning to recognize all the constellations and bright stars	Watching TV together	Cooking an exciting meal together
Buying a new record	Working for a political candidate	Riding bikes in the country
Canoeing	Going to a little drugstore for the best chocolate shake in town	Painting the house
Doing exercises (Yoga, isometrics, dance, calisthenics)	Making home-made pizzas and throwing lots of stuff on them	Taking a drive in the country

Calling up an old mutual friend on the phone long distance	Joining a new group or club together	Browsing in a bookstore
Visiting a brand new intersting place for a day	Hanging out in a new coffee shop, talking and trying out new coffees	Looking at slides, photos, or home movies
Making or planning home improvements	Eating pizza (at home or at a restaurant)	Cooking something we've never cooked before
Going horseback riding	Going swimming in the nude	Washing the car
Going on a shopping spree	Watching late movies on TV and cuddling during the commercials	Getting up to see the sunrise
Inviting someone new over for dinner or drinks	Inventing a language of our own	Reading science fiction or mysteries out loud in bed at night

Playing with pets	Bar hopping	Going to a friendly bar together or with friends, drinking lots of beer
aking a picnic lunch to a nearby state park and going hiking. Together or with friends	Spending a romantic evening alone (dinner, candlelight, music)	Buying new home decorations (sculptures, paintings, ceramics, etc.)
Taking a walk in the woods	Going to a party	Eating breakfast out
Going to a bar and talking (and playing pool sometimes)	Doing a jigsaw or crossword puzzle	Going to the library; browsing through the books and records together
Going to a play	Doing the bills together	Sunbathing
Inviting old friends over for Sunday brunch	Reading poetry out loud	Watercoloring or fingerpainting together

Poking around in secondhand or antique shops	Going swimming	Going to an auction
Eating and talking together	Going caving	Going dancing (ballroom, folkdancing, square dancing)
Going to a motel for the night	Giving a party	Going to the opera
Arranging and taking pictures	Going out late at night and buying ½ dozen all different donuts. Going home and sitting in the dark and trying to figure out by taste which one you've got	Making a collage
Visiting friends	Going out to eat	Turning down the sound on the TV and making up funny scripts
Going to church	Planning a patio barbecue	Playing in the snow or leaves

Backpacking	Going to a movie together	Planning a family reunion
Reading in bed together	Meeting for lunch or coffee during the day	Gossiping
Baking bread	Having a family cookout in the park	Working on crafts together. (tie-dying, pottery, candle making, etc.)
Playing badminton	Listening to music	Flying a kite
Fishing	Exploring new places, places you'd never usually go (junkyard, new bars, new areas of town)	Talking about day-to-day happenings
Gardening together	Making love	Going picnicking

REFERENCES

Alexander, J. F. Defensive and supportive communications in family systems. *Journal of Marriage and the Family,* 1973, *35,* 613-617.

Azrin, N. H., Naster, B. J. & Jones, R. Reciprocity counseling: A rapid learning-based procedure for marital counseling. *Behaviour Research and Therapy,* 1973, *11,* 365-382.

Bach, G. R. & Wyden, P. *The intimate enemy: How to fight fair in love and marriage.* New York: Avon Books, 1969.

Baskin, H. & Kiel-Friedman, S. *I've had it, You've had it.* New York: Nash Publishing Corp., 1974.

Bateson, G., Jackson, D. D., Haley, J. & Weakland, J. Toward a theory of schizophrenia. *Behavioral Science,* 1956, *1,* 251-264.

Bernstein, D. A. & Borkovec, T. D. *Progressive relaxation training: A manual for the helping professions.* Champaign, IL: Research Press Co., 1973.

Birchler, G. R., Weiss, R. L. & Vincent, J. P. Multimethod analysis of social reinforcement exchange between maritally distressed and nondistressed spouse and stranger dyads. *Journal of Personality and Social Psychology,* 1975, *31* (2), 349-360.

Burgess, E. W. & Cottrell, L. S. *Predicting success or failure in marriage.* New York: Prentice-Hall, 1939.

Burgess, E. W., Locke, J. J. & Thomes, M. M. *The family.* New York: Van Nostrand Reinhold, 1971.

Comfort, A. *The joy of sex.* New York: Crown Publishing, Inc., 1972.

Desport, J. L. *Children of divorce.* New York: Dolphin Books, 1962.

Downing, G. *Massage book.* Berkeley, CA: Book Works Publishing Co., 1972. Distributed by Random House.

Fuller, J. *Space.* Greenwich, CT: Fawcett Publications, Inc., 1973.

Gagné, R. M. Curriculum research and the promotion of learning. In R. E. Stake (Ed.), *AERA curriculum monograph series No. 1.* Chicago: Rand McNally, 1967.

Gergen, K. *The psychology of behavior exchange.* Reading, MA: Addison-Wesley Publishing Co., 1969.

Gunther, B. *Sense relaxation below your mind.* New York: Macmillan, Inc., 1968.

Haley, J. Research on family patterns: An instrument measurement. *Family Process,* 1964, *3* (1), 41-65.

Haley, J. Speech sequences of normal and abnormal families with two children present. *Family Process,* 1967, *6* (1), 81-97.

Hall, J. Decisions, decisions, decisions. *Psychology Today,* November 1971, 51-88.

Halverson, C. F. & Waldrop, M. F. Maternal behavior toward own and other preschool children: The problem of "ownness." *Child Development,* 1970, *41,* 839-45.

Hartman, W. E. & Fithian, M. A. *Treatment of sexual dysfunction: A bio-psycho-social approach.* Long Beach, CA: Center for Marital and Sexual Studies, 5199 E. Pacific Coast Highway, 1972.

Jacob, T. Family interaction in disturbed and normal families: A methodological and substantive review. *Psychological Bulletin,* 1975, *82,* 33-65.

Jacob, T. & Davis, J. Family interaction as a function of experimental task. *Family Process,* 1973, *12* (4), 415-427.

Krantzler, M. *Creative divorce.* New York: New American Library, 1974.

Lederer, W. J. & Jackson, D. D. *The mirages of marriage.* New York: W. W. Norton and Co., 1968.

Locke, H. J. *Prediction adjustment in marriage: A comparison of a divorced and happily married group.* New York: Holt, Rinehart and Winston, 1961.

LoPiccolo, J. & Lobitz, W. C. Behavior therapy of sexual dysfunction. In Leo A. Hamerlynck, Lee C. Handy and Eric J. Mash (Eds.), *Behavior change: The Fourth Banff Conference* on behavior modification. Champaign, IL: Research Press Co., 1973.

Masters, W. H. & Johnson, V. *Human sexual inadequacy.* Boston: Little, Brown and Co., 1971.

Mayer, M. F. *Divorce and annulment in the Southern states.* New York: Arc Books, Inc., 1971.

Mehrabian, A. *Nonverbal communication.* Chicago: Aldine Publishing Co., 1972.

Mischel, W. *Personality and assessment.* New York: John Wiley and Sons, 1968.

Mitchell, H. E., Bullard, J. W. & Mudd, E. H. Areas of marital conflict in successfully and unsuccessfully functioning families. *Journal of Health and Human Behavior,* 1962, *3* (2), 88-93.

Olson, D. H. & Ryder, R. G. Inventory of marital conflicts (IMC): An experimental interaction procedure. *Journal of Marriage and the Family,* 1970, 443-448.

Otto, H. *Fantasy encounter games.* N. Hollywood, CA: Wilshire Book Co., 1974.

Raush, H. L., Barry, W. A., Hertel, R. K. & Swain, M. A. *Communication, conflict and marriage.* San Francisco: Josey-Bass, Inc., 1974.

Rappaport, A. F. & Harrell, J. A behavioral-exchange model for marital counseling. *Family Coordinator,* 1972, *2,* 203-212.

Riskin, J. & Faunce, E. E. An evaluative review of family interaction research. *Family Process,* 1972, *11* (4), 365-455.

Ryder, R. G. Husband-wife dyads versus married strangers. *Family Process,* 1968, *7,* 233-237.

Schutz, W. C. *FIRO: A three dimensional theory of interpersonal behavior.* New York: Holt, Rinehart and Winston, 1958.

Speer, D. C. Marital dysfunctionality and two-person non-zero-sum game behavior. *Journal of Personality and Social Psychology,* 1972, *21* (1), 18-24.

Strodtbeck, F. L. Husband-wife interaction over revealed differences. *American Sociological Review,* 1951, *16,* 468-473.

Stuart, R. B. Operant interpersonal treatment for marital discord. *Journal of Consulting and Clinical Psychology,* 1969, *33* (6), 675-682.

219

Thibaut, J. W. & Kelley, H. H. *The social psychology of groups.* New York: John Wiley and Sons, 1959.

Uhr, L. M. Personality changes during marriage. Doctoral dissertation, University of Michigan, 1957.

Weiss, R. L. *Marital separation.* New York: Basic Books, Inc., 1975.

Weiss, R. L., Hops, H. & Patterson, G. R. A framework for conceptualizing marital conflict: A technology for altering it, some data for evaluating it. In Leo A. Hamerlynck, Lee C. Handy and Eric J. Mash (Eds.), *Behavior change: The Fourth Banff Conference on behavior modification.* Champaign, IL: Research Press Co., 1973.

Wheeler, M. *No fault divorce.* Boston: Beacon Press, 1975.

Winter, W. D., Ferreira, A. J. & Bowers, M. Decision-making in married and unrelated couples. *Family Process,* 1973, *12,* 83-94.